101-A:Pet Sitting Business

Workbook to Conquer Success

DEBORAH LAUGHLIN

Cover By: Donna Casey, www.digitaldonna.com.
Book Design By: Go Published, www.gopublished.com

Library of Congress Control Number: 2011960618
ISBN-13: 978-1-468-13951-8

LETTER FROM THE AUTHOR

Welcome, and thank you for investing in my
Step-by-Step
"A-101: Pet Sitting Business
Workbook to Conquer Success"

Pet Sitting by House Calls, Inc. was founded in 1981 so that pets could stay in the comfort of their homes while giving owners the ability to travel worry free. Servicing over 10,000 customers, House Calls, Inc. is a professional, successful, profitable and dependable pet and home sitting service.

Throughout the years, I have been asked to write a book with instructions on how to start a successful pet sitting business. This book shares proven steps, key objectives and the valuable resources one needs to start and operate a successful business.

Sincerely,
Deborah Laughlin
CEO / Founder
House Calls, Inc.
Pet Sitting & Home Care Services
http://HouseCalls4Pet.com
http://101PetSitting.com

Table of Contents

101-A: Pet Sitting Business: Workbook to Conquer Success

101-B Workbook to Owning a Pet Sitting Business (and) Using Independent Contractors

101-C: Workbook to Running a Successful Pet Sitting Business

Acknowledgements

Along the way I did have the help and support of the wonderful people in my life and I would like to thank them.

Linda Gonzalez and Daphne Poh who helped to write and organize the first House Calls, Inc. company guidelines.

Katie Mason, my daughter, who took on the tremendous task of merging all my notes with the company guidelines over the years. Along with the task of proof reading the manuscript and helping to organizing the order the book.

Tracy Laughlin, my daughter, who helped to keep me motivated and kept me on task as I worked my way towards completing this book.

Attorney Jeffery Mc Clure and Attorney Pat Leong who supported me through the long, arduous battle with the State of California to legitimize my company's use of Independent Contractors.

My husband Doug and son Andrew for being so patient while I embarked on this journey.

Introduction

Welcome to the "101-A:Pet Sitting Business Workbook to Conquer Success", designed specifically to assist you in successfully developing and running your very own professional pet sitting service. The format gives you plenty of the necessary room to write and record your progress as you take the steps to ensure your success.

The beginning of this book will present the basics, and all parts contain clearly written steps for the tasks you will need to perform. Use each section as a stepping-stone to success in developing your business.

A Note from Debbie

I grew up in a home where animals were always present. One of my earlier memories is that of holding a cracker in one hand and the tail of George, my family's tomcat, in the other. (George *was* a very patient and trusting fellow.) My cousin Grady's menagerie included an alligator, gerbils, mice and a lizard, all of which I loved to visit. Also, there were stray cats that made their home near the creek that flowed behind our home. My lively interest in these feral felines cost me a painful series of rabies shots.

When I outgrew my teddy bear at age 12, I found my best friend; a Cocker Spaniel and Pekingese mix, named *Sniffles*. When I moved to my first apartment, which did not allow pets, I was so lonely without my friend. Doug, then my fiancé and now my husband, helped relieve my loneliness with some gifts: first there was "*Temba*", the gerbil; then "*Tweety*", the yellow parakeet; and then "*Bruno*", the Pekingese.

In 1972, I took a trip with some friends and put *Bruno* in a kennel. He got so depressed that he did not eat for the entire week that I was gone. I vowed I would never again put a pet of mine in a kennel again. Married to Doug, who was in the military, meant a lot of traveling. All too often, airlines would not allow us to take our crew of creatures. Even if they were allowed to come along, the travel was disturbing for them. By 1979, Doug and I had two children, that we took with us on our trips to the Midwest to visit our families and relatives. To care for our pets, we hired the boy next door who had always shown an interest in them. He did a great job giving each animal the attention and food needed. However, I could tell by the muddy paw prints across my floors and carpeting that he was not used to caring for a home.

Shortly after, a few pieces of the pet/home care puzzle started to fall into place. First, because I wanted to work at home while raising my small children, and I had taken several classes at the local college on starting and running a small business. Second, while waiting in a veterinarian's office, I read an article about a woman in San Francisco who walked people's dogs in the middle of the day. If people would pay her to walk their dogs while they were at work, why wouldn't people pay me to care for their pets and homes while on vacation or business trips? I was sure of the answer to that question, and I began to ask more questions.

- Were there other such services in the area?

- What did the future of the pet-service industry hold?

- In what location would this service best be sold to the public?

Then I applied for, and received a scholarship to attend a six-month entrepreneur program offered by Advocates for Women. What I learned in that program kept me headed in the right direction, and Advocates for Women provided much of the "pat-on-the-back" support I needed. By the end of the program, we relocated our family to an area we thought would be good for my fledgling business. In June of 1981, I began my advertising campaign and the history of my pet-sitting career.

Part 1
Background

History of Debbie's Pet-Sitting Business

On June 20th, 1981 I registered the first customer for House Calls. My pet and home sitting business was then a one-person operation. For a full year, I acted on a daily basis as secretary, answering service, bookkeeper, sales person, and caretaker of the pets and homes entrusted to House Calls. Then, I began contracting work out to other caretakers who lived in cities farther away from my home-based office. As word of the service spread, additional caretakers were brought on to help during holiday rushes and summer vacations. By 1985, the business had outgrown the home office and moved to a leased space in San Ramon, CA where several people took turns staffing the office. However, as the scheduling and tracking of assignments continued to grow, it became evident that one person was needed to be responsible for office functions at all times. So, beginning in the summer of 1986, the office was run by one person with an assistant, while ten caretakers were kept busy making the actual service calls.

In the spring of 1988, I moved the office back to my home. This way, I could spend more time during non-office hours developing the business while still being with my family. With the aid of a new computer, the company's customer program was developed to handle customer's bookings, caretaker's schedules, and bookkeeping for the growing business. In 1989, the business was restructured, and became the S Corporation, **House Calls Inc**., Pet & Home Services. The company's business forms and sales materials were redesigned; a newsletter for customers was developed, and the company sold its first license to operate a branch in another area. Sales volume increased 41% over 1988, and the company needed almost thirty caretakers during its peak seasons. The 1990s began with the opening of several-licensed **House Calls Inc.,** offices in California.

Disclaimer of Endorsement

Any information obtained from this book pertaining to a specific commercial product, process or service does not constitute or imply an endorsement by the writers of this book of the product, process, or service, or its producer or provider. The views and opinions expressed in any referenced document do not necessarily state or reflect those of the writers of the book, the state of California or the United States Government.

Disclaimer of Liability

Neither the writer of this book, nor the United States Government, makes any warranty, expressed or implied, including warranties of merchantability and fitness for a particular purpose, or assumes any legal liability for the accuracy, completeness or usefulness of any information from this book or any reference to it.

Copyright

Legalese

This publication is designed to provide information in regard to the subject matter covered. It is sold with the understanding that the publisher is not engaged in rendering legal, accounting or other professional services. If legal advice or other expert assistance is required, the services of a competent professional person should be sought.

House Calls, Inc. may have patents, patent applications, trademarks, service marks, copyrights, or other intellectual property rights covering subject matter in this document. Except as expressly provided in any written agreement from House Calls, Inc., the furnishing of this document does not give you any license to these patents, trademarks, service marks, copyrights, or other property.

Part 2
The Business Plan

Knowing Yourself

There are various aspects to starting a business. Each step you take will affect the next step. Look at each step you take from all aspects of the business. Knowing what kind of person you are; your likes and dislikes; successes and failures; wants and needs will be very helpful when you create your business. You can use all of that knowledge to mold your business into the type of business that best suits you.

You will come to understand and know yourself by mapping out a Game Plan. The plan will be determined by where you see yourself and your business from the onset through the development stage and ultimate success. Organizing and prioritizing will not only help you to see the light at the end of the tunnel, but will also help you to build an enduring, satisfying, successful and profitable business.

Before opening the doors to **House Calls Inc.**, I returned to college, taking Small Business classes such and attending Small Business Administration workshops. While doing this I was also writing a business plan, working with SCORE, and volunteering in a veterinarian's office to learn first aid and more about people and pets interactions. Over the years, I have continued my education through attending a variety of classes covering topics such as computer programming, new computer software applications, computer anxiety and time management.

The following sections in this workbook will help you to create a Game Plan. Take your time and complete each of the following sections. They will assist you in understanding who you are, the process to starting your business, how to set your goals for the road to success and the means to analyze your success.

Dare to be an Entrepreneur

- Do you like to make your own decisions?

- Do you enjoy being challenged and do you thrive on competition?

- Are you outgoing by nature?

- Can you put yourself in the other person's shoes?

- Are you honest and ethical?

- Do you have will power and self-discipline?

- Do you get things done on time and plan ahead?

If you said *yes* to all of the above and you are willing to work hard and long hours (12 to 16 hours a day, probably 6 days a week, and possibly on holidays), you may be a prime candidate to start your own successful business. The secret ingredient in the formula for a successful small business is your desire to be an *obsessed owner*, one willing to put in the time and energy needed to get the job done and finish the day, still full of enthusiasm.

It is likely that running your own business will be harder than working at a regular job. Studies have demonstrated that most entrepreneurs are not primarily motivated by the desire to make money. Their satisfactions lie more in the areas of independence, power over the future, and the pleasure of accomplishing all goals.

Whether a business succeeds or fails frequently depends on having a steady cash flow. A smart entrepreneur is very conservative and reserves every bit of cash that's available for those dry periods. Giving into the temptation to expand too quickly or show off your sudden profits can and will lead to failure!

Reality of Ownership

Owning your own business while working at home has personal, professional and financial benefits. Let us compare the advantages to the disadvantages of starting your own business.

ADVANTAGES

- You are your own boss with no one to report to but yourself. You are responsible for the success.

- You can work at your own speed.

- Your schedule will be flexible. You can structure your work hours to coincide with your home life and its responsibilities.

- You reap the profits from your hard work.

- Your business may provide security or add security for you and your family.

- You will not face forced retirement.

DISADVANTAGES

- You are responsible for any failure.

- You may work during all your waking hours. Work is money.

- You will have no paid vacations; in fact you may have no vacation at all for a few years.

- You will have no weekly paycheck or fringe benefits.

- You may have less time to spend with your family.

- If the business fails, your savings and property may be eaten up by debts, leaving nothing for retirement.

Your Strong Points

One question asked frequently is, "How do I determine what area I should start a business in?" Here is a quick formula to help you find an area where you are best suited.

YOUR LIFE IN FIVE-YEAR INTERVALS

Fill out the following Success Chart. The results will provide information regarding your marketable skills.

1. List each success or accomplishment in the second column.

2. Enter the year(s) in that they took place in the first column.

3. Place the skills or experiences gained from the successes and accomplishments in the third column.

   Note: Take the time to carefully consider the satisfactions and rewards obtained by each experience. These should also be listed in the third column.

4. It is a good idea to consider negative experiences.

   Example: *You hated selling Girl Scout cookies. You should ask yourself if this typifies your attitude toward selling, and if so, you might want to stay out of this field. Place these negative experiences in the fourth column.*

Game Plan Table

Years	Successes & Accomplishments	Experience Gained & Rewards/Satisfactions	Negative Experiences

When you have determined the type of small business that is suited to you, ask yourself each of the questions on the following page and be very *thorough* in your answers.

What Best Describes Me

This exercise will help you to design your business around your strengths and likes, while being fully responsible for the additional roles necessary for a successful business!

Check off the role that best describes you, by using the chart from the previous page:

Entrepreneur

Technician

Manager

Entrepreneur

- Creative and inventive.

- Enjoys taking risks and making decisions.

- Typically does not like being in a rut.

- Self- starter and a visionary.

Technician

- Someone who is an expert at a particular task or discipline; engineer, designer, scientist, or salesperson.

- Someone that likes to go narrow and deep, and take a singular direction.

Manager

- Someone who really enjoys managing people, organizing, and administration.

- Someone who enjoys multi-tasking.

The Business Plan

Complete your business plan before you get too involved in your new business. Many entrepreneurs take business plans too lightly.

- A business plan should be a living document that you both use and learn from.

- A business plan is a promise to yourself; if you don't know where you're going you might not get there.

- A business plan forces you to evaluate if your product or service will satisfy a need. It provides a roadmap to operate your company.

Research is an essential part of the planning process. While it may seem time-consuming, it is a wise investment of time and will prevent problems down the road. To help gain experience you could volunteer at a local veterinarian's office. You will see how pet owners react to leaving their pet in someone else's care, and you will also learn first aid procedures. Work for another pet-sitting company and learn the strengths and weaknesses of that company's system. Experience is of the utmost.

The following pages will walk you through preparing the professional pet-sitting business plan.

Start up Resources

Small Business Administration program is designed to help small businesses succeed and offers many resources. Please contact the Small Business Administration "S.B.A.", Answer Desk at 800-U ASK SBA or *www.sba.gov*.

SCORE helps small businesses succeed. SCORE "Counselors to America's Small Business" is the best source of free and confidential small business advice to help you build your business—from idea to start-up to success. SCORE's extensive, national network of 10,500 retired and working volunteers are experienced entrepreneurs and corporate managers/executives. These volunteers provide free business counseling and advice as a public service to all types of businesses, in all stages of development. SCORE is a resource partner with the Small Business Administration. *www.score.org*

Welcome Business is a website dedicated to the success of your new venture. Welcome Business USA offers you a wealth of resources - how-to articles, FREE business counseling and special discounts and offers from featured vendors - to assist you with dealing with the various issues you will face in navigating your business towards success. Welcome Business is partnered with SCORE. *www.welcomebusiness.com*

Internal Revenue Service offers small business and self-employed online classes on a variety of topics for small businesses. Employment Taxes, Employer ID Numbers, links to broad range of resources across federal and state agencies. *www.irs.gov/businesses /small/index.html*

Your state web site may offer everything you need to know about starting, and operating, a business in your state.

Not understanding the law does not exempt you from penalties and interest charged by federal and state agencies if you do not follow the rules. Save time and money by understanding employment taxes both Federal and State for your business.

Create a monthly, quarterly and yearly check list or reminders system for federal and state due dates. All forms to Federal and State agencies being sent by US Mail should be sent certified to avoid receiving late fees years later. Always place your Employer ID or Federal ID number, with the form number and due date on all payments made by check even if sent with a form!

Additional Resources:

Nolo-Law for All: For over 30 years, **N.O.L.O.** has published the most reliable do-it-yourself legal and business tools available. N.O.L.O.'s more than 300 books, software and eProducts are clearly written and regularly updated. These products help you understand and tackle your affairs without hiring a pricey professional.

> www.nolo.com
>
> www.uslegalforms.com
>
> www.uslegalchecks.com

Entrepreneur.com: A tool designed to save you the time and expense of creating business documents from scratch. You can download and customize each form according to your needs, and immediately put them to work in your business. *www.entrepreneur.com*

CPA Directory: Nationwide directory of Accountants, Bookkeepers & CPAs. CPA license verification, Information on Tax & Accounting issues. *www.cpadirectory.com*

Pre-Start-up Checklist

The following items will give you an idea of the issues you will need to consider, and the steps to take in order to start your own business.

- Attend Business Start up classes and workshops
- Identify market
- Check for availability of your chosen company name
- Research market
- Research your industry and the competition
- Research potential vendors and suppliers
- Inventory control
- Research and analyze the location and space for the business
- Pricing
- Ability to raise capital
- Determine start-up and operating costs
- Assess the ability to make the business profitable
- Assess financial position and resources
- Determine potential sources of financing (self, friends, family, equity, debt)
- Calculate and prepare revenue and cash flow projections
- Find an attorney, an accountant, and an insurance professional
- Personal liability of owner
- Control of the business
- Marketing plan
- Service plan
- Continuity of the business
- Tax considerations
- Choose the legal form of your business.

Choosing the Legal Form for your Business

One of the most important decisions that organizers of a small business enterprise must make is whether to set up the business as a

- Sole Proprietorship

- Partnership

- Corporation.

A comparison of the advantages and disadvantages of these three major forms of business organization follows:

Start-up Costs

Some basic costs such as rent and the cost of acquiring inventory will vary whether you are a sole proprietorship, a partnership or a corporation. Other costs will also vary especially legal fees involved in setting up your business.

Sole Proprietorship: This is the least costly way to start a business. You can form a sole proprietorship by finding a location and opening the door for business. There are the usual fees for registering your business name and for legal work in changing zoning restrictions and obtaining necessary licenses. Attorney's fees for starting your business will be less than for the other forms because there is less preparation of documents required.

Partnership: You can form a partnership simply by an oral agreement between two or more persons, but this is not recommended. Legal fees for drawing a partnership agreement are higher than those for a sole proprietorship, but may be lower than for incorporating. However, you would be wise to consult an attorney to have a partnership agreement drawn up, to help resolve future disputes.

A partnership agreement should include the following:

- The type of business
- Amount invested by each partner
- Divisions of profit or loss
- Compensations to each partner
- Provisions for drawing salaries by partners

- Distribution of assets in event of dissolution

- Duration of partnership

- Provisions for dissolving the business

- Provisions for withdrawals or admissions of additional partners

- Procedure for dispute-settlement

- Restrictions on individual authority, especially regarding expenditures

- Settlements in event of death or incapacity of one partner

Corporation: You can incorporate without the help of an attorney, but you would be unwise to do so. You may think a small family corporation does not need an attorney, but an attorney can save the members of a family corporation from hard feelings and family squabbles down the road. Attorney's fees may run high, if organization problems are complex. The corporate form is usually the most costly to organize.

Control of the Business

Sole Proprietorship You have absolute authority over all business decisions.

Partnership Control of the business is shared with your partners, which may lead to disputes. A partnership agreement could be helpful in solving possible disputes. However, you still are responsible for your partner's business actions, as well as your own.

Corporation Control depends on stock ownership. If you have majority stock ownership, you are able to make policy decisions. Control is exercised through regular board of directors meetings and annual stockholders' meetings. Records must be kept in order to document decisions made by the board of directors. Small, closely held corporations can operate more informally, but record keeping cannot be eliminated. Officers of a corporation can be liable to stockholders for improper actions.

Tax Considerations

Sole Proprietorship and Partnership: All net income is taxable to the sole proprietorship or to the partnership according to each partner's share of ownership. Your tax rate depends on your income bracket. You may be able to deduct from your gross income some personal expenses that are directly related to your business. Some examples are:

- Personal car expenses to the extent used in the business

- A share of expenses if your business is located in your home

Corporation: There are two ways to tax a corporation: (1) as a straight corporation and (2) as a Subchapter S corporation.

As a straight corporation, profits are taxed at corporate rates that are graduated from 22% on the first $25,000 of income to 48% of income over $25,000. Salaries of officers are deductible expenses and therefore reduce corporate profit subject to income tax. However, salaries of officers are subject to individual income tax. If salaries appear too high, the IRS may treat the excess as a dividend. This means double taxation because the same money is taxed as a part of the corporate profit and as income to individuals.

If you are a Subchapter S corporation, you are taxed in the same way as a sole proprietorship or partnership. In order to qualify as a Subchapter S corporation, you must meet the following requirements:

- Have individual shareholders

- Have not more than 10 shareholders

- Have no shareholders who are nonresident aliens

- Have only one class of stock

- Have not more than 80 percent of gross receipts from outside the United States

- Have not more than 20 percent of corporation gross receipts from royalties, rents, dividends, interest, annuities, and gains on sales or exchange of stock or securities.

Ability to Raise Capital

Sole Proprietorship and Partnership: The source of capital is usually limited to personal assets of the proprietor or partner. The ability to get credit depends on personal reputation of the proprietor or partners. Third parties cannot invest in the business without incurring responsibilities for business debts.

Corporation: A corporation can theoretically sell stock to raise capital. Practically speaking, there is no market for stock in small corporations, except through friends or relatives. You may be limited to the personal resources and credit of the owners.

Continuity of the Business

Sole Proprietorship: If you are disabled, the business will falter unless family, friends, or employees are willing and able to substitute for you. Death of a sole proprietor means the end of the business, but your heirs can inherit the assets of the business. Your heirs can start a new business using the same assets and locations, providing your creditors are paid.

Partnership: If one partner is disabled, the other may be able to fill in until the disabled partner recovers. One partner cannot sell his share in a partnership without getting the consent of his partners. Death dissolves a partnership automatically. Heirs of a partner inherit his share of the Partnership assets. Without a partnership agreement, the heirs often have to sue to enforce their legal rights.

Corporation: A corporation is a separate legal entity. Its existence is not affected by death or disability of shareholders. Shares of stock can be sold if one owner wants to leave the business. On the death of a shareholder, his stock goes to his heirs.

Personal Liability of Owners

If you are borrowing from a bank, SBA or other lending institutions, personal guarantees of all principals and their spouses will be required. Certain types of liability can be insured against, such as liability for accidents to customers on your premises. The following is concerned with personal liability for trade debts.

Sole Proprietorship: All personal assets are available to creditors to satisfy claims against you. This does not generally mean creditors can sell your home. If you and your spouse jointly own your home, your spouse is not liable for your business debts, and his or her interest in the house is not divisible. A creditor can obtain a judgment, which is good for 20 years. In that period, your spouse may die, leaving you sole owner. You and your spouse may divorce, or more commonly, you may wish to sell and move elsewhere. If any of the above happens, you would have to come to terms with your creditors.

Partnership: The general rule is that all personal assets are on the line for business debts incurred by you or your partner. This may include your home, in which case the personal liability is the same as for a sole proprietorship unless your spouse is a partner. If you have more money than your partner, you may have to bear the brunt of business debts, even though the partnership agreement says you will split debts fifty-fifty. A partnership agreement does not bind third parties who are not aware of it.

Corporation: If you invest an amount of money in a corporation, you can lose only that amount plus the time and effort you put into the business. Creditors of corporations cannot reach your personal assets for corporation debts.

Defining Your Business

Identify Market

Who are your customers?	List Customers
Individuals	
Organizations	
Businesses	

Research Market

Who are your customers?	List Customers
Individuals	
Organizations	
Businesses	
How will your service compare	**What is the value-ad for your service**
Location	**Enter address**
County	
City	
Street	

Marketing Plan

How will you advertise your service	Answer
What image do you wish to project	
Do you have a motto, symbol, or trademark	
How do you provide your service	

Pricing

How will you advertise your service	Answer
Do you understand your initial set-up costs	
Raw materials cost	
Labor Cost	
Overhead Cost (breakdown)	
Administrative Cost	
Advertising and Selling	
What is your markup or profit margin	

Office Space Working from Home

How do you present your service	Answer
Home Address P.O. Box/Box Rental with Suite Address	
How much room do you need Storage Office	

Cash Flow

How will your customers pay you	Answer
When	
What will you do if they don't	

Service Plan

What is your basic service plan	Answer
Are there extras	
Do you guarantee your product or service	
For how long	

Inventory Control

What Purchasing information do you have	Answer
Do you have a purchasing schedule	
Do you know your suppliers	
Do you have alternative suppliers	

Business Start-up Checklist

The following table lists the tasks to be taken care, after the pre-start-up items have been completed. This will help ensure a successfully business setup.

Check	Business Start-up Check List
	File fictitious Business Name
	Apply for a City Business License
	Establish a Business Bank Account
	Establish a Pet-sitter Trust Account if you are going to retain independent contractors to pet-sit
	Implement a Financial Plan
	Establish record-keeping procedures
	Install a telephone system (business phone line, voice mail system, cell phone, pager, etc.)
	Implement a computer system (and Internet access)
	Install security software and power protection
	Install an office database & scheduling software
	Install Accounting Software
	Buy business Insurance
	Acquire Professional Associates, (Business Lawyer, CPA, Insurance Agent)
	Set up operational procedures and policies, such as payroll
	Order raw materials (office supplies/furniture)
	Design Forms and Agreements
	Purchase a Postage System
	Recruit and hire
	Establish and market a presence (register a website domain name, promotional products, etc.)
	Execute a Marketing Plan
	Join your local Chamber of Commerce
	Join your local professional pet-sitting organizations
	Get listed with the Better Business Bureau www.bbb.org
	Get a professional Logo design and Trademark
	Register your Logo and Name with your State and Federal Agencies
	Enquire about local advertising and listings

Check	Business Start-up Check List
	Get your own Domain Name and register it for several years
	Get a hosting company for a local small business website with unique IP address
	Set Up email address using your domain name. which looks more professional
	Website: Create a business Website. If you do not know how to make a "good website" hire a web designer for a nominal fee. The website will be the first impression of your business to online. www.petcalls.biz
	Google: Get listed on Google Maps (free) www.google.com/local/add/login
	Super Pages: Get you business listed (free & fee options) https://superpages.com/spweb/products/business-listing
	Update your listing with inforUSA.com and Acxion http://list.inforusa.com/dbupdate.htm http://bcb.acxion.com/start.pl
	Yahoo Local get listed (free & fee options) http://searchmarketings.yahoo.com/local/business.php
	Dmoz.org find a category that matches yours and get listed www.dmoz.org
	MSN get listed via localize.co www.localeze.om/manage/
	Yellowpages.com get listed (free & fee options) www.yellowpages.com
	Face book Create a fan page for your business www.facebook.com
	LinkedIn Add your profile and business www.linkedin.com
	Yelp Add your business www.yelp.com

You might be able to save yourself time with RegisterLocal.com offered by Local Launch which offers to keep your business profile information up to date with various Yellow page, local search providers and data companies who provide information to various local outlets.

Start-up Expenses Questionnaire

1. Do you need printed business cards, brochures, contracts, stationery, invoices, wrapping paper, shopping bags, etc?

2. Do you need to buy a mailing list or lists?

3. Do you need to rent workspace, furniture, or a computer?

4. Do you need a separate phone line for the business?

5. What are the advertising rates in the local newspapers, yellow pages, movie theaters, and TV and radio stations? Can you arrange to have a promotional article written about your new business?

6. Will you need a telephone answering service, voice mail or answering machine, cell phone or pager?

7. Will you need professional services (accountant, attorney, consultant, etc.)?

8. Do you need a local business license? What are the fees? Have you filed your fictitious business name and paid the fee?

9. Do you need to pay for insurance and bonding premiums?

Think of every hidden expense and write it down. Talk with people in similar businesses and ask them what expenses, including the unexpected, are likely to crop up. Draw up a budget and compare it with your cash on hand to estimate how much capital you need to raise.

Note: Budgeting software is included in many accounting programs.

Why Computerize Your Business

There are many reasons why one should computerize their business. The businesses that succeed are the ones who offer superior service and stay on top of their finances. For example: When a business is computerized and the customer calls to book pet-sitting, it is easy to pull up their name to see if they are an existing client, which pet-sitter services them, their pets' names, if they owe money, and more. Now your interaction with that customer just got much more personal, making them feel even more confident with your services. In fact, tracking where your money is coming from and where it's going is one of the most important steps you can take to help ensure your business becomes a success story, not a statistic. A computer system will save you time and make it easier to do your budgeting, payroll, tax forms, mailing lists, etc. Having a computer as well as a paper system for your business will help to assure you of accuracy and efficiency. You must have the proper software for this to work smoothly, and your computer must be up to date enough to hold the program and any information you put into it. It is a must to get an easy to perform daily back up system for your system incase of computer failure.

Some sort of Office suite software can help you work more efficiently. Office suite software makes it easy to share data across applications, as they contain the most sophisticated versions of a company's word processor, database, and spreadsheet programs. Purchasing a suite that contains many such task-oriented applications is much cheaper then purchasing each application separately. Other advantages of this software is its cohesiveness, allowing you to easily switch from application to application by using your own customized toolbar, and consistency, meaning that you can do the same thing the same way in different programs, making it easier to learn and use. All of the different suite systems out there offer a variety of help tools to get you through any task you may be trying to accomplish. The program reduces the number of steps it would normally take to finish a task.

Computerizing your business will help you work more productively, make informed decisions and exceed customer expectations.

Pet Sitting Software Office Manager by:

House Calls, Inc. has a custom computer program in
Access for the Microsoft Office developed as House Calls has
grown and used by all House Calls Offices.
It does everything except walk the dog!
Contact me directly for a personal on line demonstration.
Debbie@housecalls4pet.com

Why Have A Web Site

A business, you should have a website. Period. No question. To have your own website gives your business invaluable advantages over the traditional modes of advertising

It is not enough to have a website. You must have a professional-looking site if you want to be taken seriously. Since many consumers now search for information online prior to making a purchase. You have one chance to make a good impression on a potential buyer

24/7 availability:

A website is available to you 24 hours a day, 7 days a week, 365 days a year. It will be your hardest working employee, never getting sick, or taking a holiday. And you can rest assured that your website is always there for you – to answer your customers' questions, or to collect their feedback on your behalf.

Make information available to work colleagues accessible from anywhere at any time. (Pages can be password protected.)

Efficient low-cost advertising:

Your website practically runs NON-STOP PROMOTIONS of your business! Your customers will always be able to obtain thorough up-to-date information about your services or products. Instead of having to rely on randomly aired TV or radio commercials, they can simply browse through your website whenever they like. Save money - Save yourself the cost of printing a full color brochure - much more can be included on your website and it can of course be updated at any time, so saving re-printing costs

Saves money:

You can save a lot of money you would have otherwise spent on print ads, brochures, coupons, flyers, specials, newsletters or mailings. What's more, updating the information on your website is always quick, easy and amazingly efficient, whereas regular renewals of printed materials can be quite expensive and time consuming. Attract new clients by putting your website address on your business card. People you don't have time to talk with at length can view your website in their own time..

Enhanced customer convenience:

Searching for businesses, products and services over the Internet is much easier and quicker than leafing through the Yellow Pages, for example. Every time a potential or an existing client wants to find out more about your business, they can easily do so, especially if you have added a "FAQ" section. Your customers can always keep in touch with you and your business, all they need to know is your website's address.

Greater reachability of your business :

Your business profile will be accessible from EVERYWHERE. No other ad medium provides such global coverage. You will not depend on restricted phone book entry presentations any more. What is more important, more and more customers are nowadays referring to the Internet when searching for products, services and businesses.

Greater possibilities for promoting your business :

People will not buy your products or services unless they know that they actually exist. You can tell your potential audience much more through a WEBSITE than you could possibly do via any print advertisements, Yellow Pages listings, or TV/radio commercials. There are no limitations as far as space, time, nationality and residency are concerned. You can say as many things as you want, to as many people as you wish. And your business representation can be as resourceful as is the Internet itself.

Saves time:

Prospective clients can learn about you and your business at any time of the day simply by visiting your website, so you won't have to be present or involved with the process in any way. The time you would otherwise have spent on answering or redirecting your customers' questions can be now saved and invested in other activities that can increase your profits and further enhance the scope of your business.

The Professional Pet-Sitting Plan

What is your vision for your pet-sitting business

What are your values as a business owner
(What is important to you about life? How do you vision Success?)

What is your company mission statement

What are your company's goals

What are your company's key objectives

KEY OBJECTIVES

List your key objectives. This unlocks the urgencies of your business and turns them into an everyday agenda. **There are three types of Key Objectives**:

Negative	Too high to attain
o	Doesn't make a difference
Positive	Empowering

After listing your key objectives, apply one of the ratings to each of them. In order to give a key objective a positive rating, it must meet the criteria below, so take your time and really think about each one.

Criteria for Empowering Objectives (Positive rating)

Answer the questions listed below. If the answer to a question is other than *yes* see if you can determine what is missing and redesign your objectives to provide it or, if appropriate, abandon it in favor of others.

Measurable: Can you tell when it has been accomplished? Is there a date by which you will have it accomplished?

Relevant: Will achieving this objective forward what my goals are in life? Will it enhance my goals in life?

Achievable: Is there some evidence that I will be able to achieve this objective, even though I might not yet see how?

Challenging: Does this objective put me at risk? Does it challenge me? Does it get me excited? Or is it simply predictable?

Committed: Am I fully committed to the outcome, regardless of what circumstances may challenge my success? Or is it just a good idea, which I'll accomplish only if everything works out?

Communicated: Is my objective written down and available? Have I communicated it to others? Have I enrolled others in sharing my commitment?

Coached: Do you have someone to support and help you achieve your objective?

With the key objectives in mind, write your empowering objectives. Limit them to five in each of three time periods.

	Objectives
1	Until the end of this year
2	Next year
3	Three to five years

	Empowering Objectives / TIME FRAME # 1
1	
2	
3	
4	
5	

	Empowering Objectives / TIME FRAME # 2
1	
2	
3	
4	
5	

	Empowering Objectives / TIME FRAME # 3
1	
2	
3	
4	
5	

Email Debbie for personal coaching services:

HouseCalls4Pet.com
101PetSitting.com

101-B Workbook to Owning a Pet Sitting Business (and) Using Independent Contractors

This book will present the basics, and all sections contain clearly written steps for the tasks you will need to perform. Use each section as a stepping-stone to success in developing your business and successfully using independent contractors.

A Note from Debbie

This manual was conceived after a long, arduous and expensive battle that I, the owner of a pet-sitting service in California, was forced to endure in order to legitimize my company's independent contractor relationships. I disproved the adage that *you can't fight City Hall*. On the contrary, I took on the state taxing authorities in a litigation that resulted in (to my knowledge) the first and only decision by an Administrative Law Judge in favor of a pet-sitting agency on this issue.

My odyssey against the State of California stands as an example of the many reasons why pet-sitting agencies that utilize independent contractors, need to ensure that they truly understand the legal and practical effect of such relationships. As a result of my experience and knowledge, I decided to publish this guide designed solely for the pet-sitting industry.

The guide is intended to provide pet-sitting agencies with a road map to successfully utilize independent contractors in their businesses. Upon reading it, the business owner should have a practical idea of how to create, implement, and perhaps most importantly, defend their independent contractor relationship.

Independent Contractors in the Pet-Sitting Industry

- **Independent contractors**

    - Benefits and risks of hiring independent contractors
    - Determining whether workers are independent contractors or employees

- **Steps to take before hiring an independent contractor**

- **Proper procedures to follow in forming an independent contractor relationship**

    - Paperwork necessary to hire an independent contractor
    - Independent contractor agreement
    - Common law factors used to determine workers' classification
    - How to meet the twenty common law factors determining
    - Worker's classification
    - Additional items used in determining workers' classification
    - Independent contractor reporting (Federal & State)
    - Paying independent contractors
    - Sample one-week tally sheet for the independent contractor to use to bill the Agency.

- **Dos and Don'ts of using independent contractors**

    - Debbie's story (case overview, lessons learned…)
    - Worksheet: Self-Audit Your Independent Contactor Relationships

Independent Contractors

Independent contractors are individuals who contract to perform services for others, without having the legal status of employees.

Many business owners think that they can properly maintain independent contractor relationships, simply by having a written agreement that designates workers as independent contractors. Smarter business owners know that this is not the case. Although the parties' understanding is one factor in properly establishing such a relationship, the real key is whether the parties treat themselves as true independent businesses.

This guide is designed around five main subject areas:

- **Legal Section**

  You need to understand the legal framework surrounding this complex issue so you can make the decisions that will enable you to properly maintain independent contractor relationships. These legal principles are presented in layperson's terms so that you can utilize your newfound understanding of the law in your business.

- **Practical Issues**

  The manual addresses the practical problems pet-sitting agencies face when establishing and maintaining independent contractor relationships. We present you with a "Dos and Don'ts list" that will help you make sense of the issues faced in maintaining a legally defensible independent contractor relationship that actually makes sense in the context of the way you do business.

- **Model Agreement**

The manual presents, and then explains, a model independent contractor agreement that has been designed specifically for the pet-sitting industry.

- **Defending the Relationship**

The manual provides you with the tools you need to respond to legal challenges to your independent contractor relationships. These challenges could arise during an employment tax audit by the state by federal taxing authorities, an unemployment benefits case, or a lawsuit.

Benefits of hiring independent contractors

Businesses can usually save money by hiring independent contractors (I.C.'s) instead of employees. In addition to salary, there are other expenses, which can add at least 20-30% to payroll costs for employees. These include:

- Federal payroll taxes
- Social Security tax
- Federal unemployment insurance tax
- State unemployment insurance
- Employee benefits
- Office space
- Workers' compensation insurance

When a company uses an I.C., they simply pay whatever the I.C. charges them for the job. During peak season you can contract the workforce quickly without cost of layoffs or firings.

Risks of hiring independent contractors

There are consequences to misclassifying as ICs workers who are legally employees. These consequences can be economically devastating. The business must pay the IRS all back taxes owed, with interest, plus a penalty of 12-35% of the tax bill. The business will also receive a state audit and be subject to fines and penalties. In addition, independent contractors can sue for negligence if they are injured on the job.

California Law

Right to Control is Key

The law presumes, until it is proven otherwise, that an employment relationship exists between a hiring company and its workers. As a result, workers will not be treated as Independent Contractors unless the company proves that they are independent contractors. The most important factor in determining whether an Independent Contractor or an Employment Relationship exists is "whether the person to whom the service is rendered has the right to control the manner and means of accomplishing the result desired" (*see S. G. Borello & Sons v. Dept. of Industrial Relations* (1989) 48 Cal.3d 341, 350. This "Right to Control" is a key theme underlying this guide because it is the lynchpin to all independent contractor relationships.

However, this does not mean that the hiring company cedes control over every aspect of the job. The hiring company is still entitled to determine what it wants as the end product. Example: if a hiring company requested a contractor to paint a building in the color of blue, they don't have to sit idly by while the contractor determines to paint it pink. The hiring company always retains the right of control over the end product to its specifications. However, it must cede the hired person's methods in producing the product.

Steps to take before hiring an Independent Contractor

When hiring an independent contractor, documents must be kept to prove the contractor is *not* an employee.

When meeting with a prospective I.C., they must fill out an independent contractor questionnaire. The questions should be designed to provide information that will establish that the I.C. is a separate business entity.

Some of the answers you need to know are:

- Does the I.C. have an assumed or a fictitious business name?
- Their businesses address and phone number
- If the I.C. holds any professional business licenses
- The number, if any, of people employed by the I.C.
- How the I.C. 's business is structured
- Contract information for any other companies the I.C. has worked for as an independent contractor
- A description of the business equipment the I.C. holds
- Does the I.C. have their own business cards, stationary, invoices, forms and other paper needs
- Type of insurance the carried by the I.C.

Note: Do not have an I.C. complete a standard employment application. This can be used later as evidence that the I.C. is in fact an employee.

Proper procedures to form an Independent Contractor Relationship

In a true independent contractor relationship, the hiring company's main interest must be in getting the contracted-for, finished product. In the pet-sitting industry, this means the Agency (hiring company) should be interested in obtaining a satisfactory pet-sitting report and not in the way that the independent contractor or Agent performed the services that resulted in the pet-sitting report.

There is a fine line between the hiring company's legitimate interest in getting what it has contracted for, and interfering in the way that the IC performs his or her services. Setting up the initial relationship is not the beginning and the end of the process. Continuous scrutiny of every aspect of the working relationship is required. Ensure that the company's interest remains focused on receiving the contracted-for product, *not* on the methods and means by which the IC creates that product.

Both Parties' Intentions and Expectations

The relationship in which the parties view themselves is very important – but not because the legal authorities will give a great deal of weight to the parties' intention to create an independent contractor relationship. Frankly, they probably won't give it any weight at all.

The parties' intent is very important, however, if both parties commit to doing everything in their power to continually reinforce the independent contractor arrangement. In this vein, the company should use opportunities that arise to remind the Agent that he or she is an independent contractor. But the hiring company should also take steps to insure that others, particularly clients, do not misunderstand the relationship between the company and the Agents. The company's promotional and marketing efforts should always emphasize that the Agents, although associated with the company for the limited purpose of providing the contracted-for services (like subcontractors), are nevertheless independent businesspersons.

The independent contractor/Agent has a corresponding duty to reinforce the relationship. The Agent must think of himself/herself as an independent businessperson. The following are some of the ways a person can establish this:

- Obtain bonding.
- Join professional associations and work towards certification in those organizations.
- Get a city or county business license.
- Open a bank account for your business.
- Actively solicit your own clients.
- Arrange for a separate telephone line for your business to be installed at your home.
- Advertise in the Yellow Pages, or at the very least, take out a white pages listing under your name, representing yourself as an independent agent.
- Build direct client relationships with clients for whom you perform pet-sitting services through the hiring company so that you are not totally dependent on the hiring company as your exclusive source of referrals.
- Invest in your own market data resources and use them when possible.
- Maintain an office in your home, or elsewhere.
- Invest in a computer and printer and prepare your pet-sitting schedules and bookkeeping in your own office.
- Buy your own business cards, indicating that you are an independent Pet Sitting Agent.
- Represent yourself to clients of the hiring company as a Professional Independent Pet Sitter.

Always conduct yourself as the independent businessperson that you are.

Integration of the Agent's Services with the Hiring Company's Business Enterprise

As you will recall, one of the factors considered by both the California and IRS tests is whether the services provided by the worker are an integral part of the hiring company's business. Admittedly, this is going to be a difficult legal test for the traditional Agency to meet when contracting with Agents on an independent contractor basis.

Deciding When to Work

Independent contractors should, above all else, retain their independence. This means that the contractor, *not the company*, decides when to work and when not to work, or whether to accept or reject a particular pet-sitting assignment. This is the biggest benefit to the independent contractor, and the biggest drawback of the relationship for the pet-sitting company. However, it is a right that cannot be ignored.

Working for Others

Nor should the company interfere with the Agent's opportunity to work for its own independent clients or with other pet-sitting firms. Often when determining whether an independent contractor or an employment relationship exists, the question is asked whether the Agent can work for more than one firm – i.e., whether the hiring company requires that the Agent works only for them. Independent businesspersons generally have the right to work for anyone they choose. Arrangements between independent businesses, that provides that one business will provide services or products exclusively to the other (so-called "exclusive dealing" contracts) are a rarity.

Progress Reports

Even when an Agent has accepted an assignment as an independent contractor, the Agent should not become accountable to the hiring company until the contract is completed. The hiring company should never require an Agent to submit reports during the course of a pet-sitting assignment. Progress reports, status reports and other systems, which require the Agent to report to the hiring company on the status of work in progress, are telltale signs of an employment relationship. They show that the hiring company is overseeing the ongoing performance of the contractor prior to completion of the contract.

Naturally, the pet-sitting company has a legitimate interest that an Agent, who has accepted an assignment, will follow client instructions for the job. Keep track of assignments *internally* to make sure that the company's commitments to clients will be met. **Example:** *a record of all outstanding assignments, noting the Agent that accepted the assignment; the date the assignment was accepted; the client's due home date and time and a note and was submitted to the client. This is a necessary and proper business practice, not an exercise of control over the way that the Agent is performing the assignments.* When discussing the assignment with the Agent, the company should limit its inquiry to whether or not the Agent will be able to meet the contract instructions from the customer and be available to complete the service dates requested and continue services until the clients' calls to state they are home. The company should not inquire about the tasks that remain to be completed; scheduling the remaining tasks; restructuring the Agent's workload; prioritizing assignments, etc. Failure to follow these rules leads to questions pertaining to the realm of responsibility of the independent contractor.

Maintaining Quality

This does not mean that the hiring company cannot safeguard its paramount interests, such as maintaining the quality of the work product provided to clients. It is the manner in which the company does so that is *all-important.*

Skill Level Required

The skill level required by a particular occupation is a factor considered in deciding whether the worker is an independent contractor. Occupations that require a high skill level fit more easily into an independent contractor analysis. Skilled workers exercise more discretion and judgment in the performance of their services than unskilled workers. Therefore, it is less likely that a person contracting for a skilled worker's services will control the methods and means used by the skilled worker to perform the services. One must be self-motivated, extremely organized, observant, and possess the people skills required to build the potential customer's confidence so they entrust their home and pets to pet sitter. The pet sitter must have knowledge of animal behavior in order to build the pet's confidence as well, to allow them enter the domain of the pet while the owner is away and administer medications. "Pet-sitting" is clearly a skilled occupation.

Training

To become a certified pet sitter, an individual can contact Pet Sitters International or The National Association of Pet Sitters **independently**. Requiring this certification or some other form of training creates a potential problem for the independent contractor relationship.

An employer-employee relationship is almost always indicated when a hiring company provides training to a worker.

1. A company would not normally hire an independent contractor if the company knew that the independent contractor did not possess the pre-requisite skills to independently perform the contracted-for services; and worse yet, the hiring company would have to spend its own time and resources to train the independent contractor to complete the project.

2. When a hiring company provides training, it is *instructing* the worker on how to perform a task, the key issue involved in the right-of-control test. To properly train someone to perform a pet-sitting service requires not just instruction on valuation theories, but also very detailed instructions on how to actually perform a pet-sitting assignment. Therefore, if the hiring company provides the training to an Agent, you can assume that the IRS and the State Agency would conclude that a valid independent contractor relationship does not exist.

Note: Should a *trainee* Agent work under the *direct supervision* of a licensed or certified Agent the obligation to control the unlicensed Agent's work would then become the responsibility of the licensed or certified Agent.

The safest way to prevent problems that might arise with this issue is to enter into independent contractor relationships *only* with duly experienced Pet Sitters. Independent contractor relationships with non-experienced Pet Sitters are not recommended and must be carefully reconsidered.

The Cost of Doing Business

The IRS and your State Agency are particularly interested in who pays the expenses incurred by the Agent in the course of performing pet-sitting services for the hiring company. An employment relationship is generally indicated if the hiring company pays for expenses. Independent businesspersons, on the other hand, take the responsibility to provide the tools necessary to conduct their businesses and pay for the expenses incurred in their businesses.

The Risk of Doing Business

Independent businesspersons are responsible for the risk of loss attributable to their business operations. On the other hand, employees are generally not liable for losses suffered by a business even if the loss is attributable to the employee's conduct. Thus, the courts and administrative agencies will scrutinize alleged independent contractor relationships to ascertain whether the worker carries a real risk of loss.

As an independent businessperson, the Agent should be able to decide for himself or herself whether using assistants will be a cost-effective way to complete a pet-sitting assignment. Of course, the Agent, not the hiring company, has the obligation to pay and provide workers' compensation insurance for his or her employees. Under California's workers' compensation laws, if the Agent was later found to be the hiring company's employee, the hiring company would be responsible for providing workers' compensation insurance to the Agent's employees. Thus, to protect itself against a potential civil liability by one of the Agent's employees, the hiring company should require the Agent to provide proof of workers' compensation insurance coverage for his or her employees.

The Agent is also responsible for supervising his or her employees to assure that a quality product is produced. The Agent still has an obligation to provide a pet-sitting bill to the customer and Agency. If the customer because of the substandard work of the Agent's employees does not pay the pet-sitting bill, the hiring company should simply turn back the pet-sitting bill to the Agent. The hiring company should never directly or indirectly become involved in supervising the Agent's employees.

Of course, the Agent must keep in mind the peculiar problems Agents now face regarding the use of Pet Sitters for contracted work accepted from an Agency.

Trading and Sharing Assignments

In some agencies, it is not unusual for Agents to "trade" or "share" assignments with other Agents who also contract with the agency. When a "trade" takes place, the second Agent agrees to perform the services that the first Agent contracted to perform, usually in exchange for receiving all or part of the first Agent's fee. In effect, the first Agent has subcontracted the assignment out.

When Agents "share" an assignment, two or more Agents agree with the company to perform the assignment, or the second Agent agrees to help the first Agent perform an assignment the first Agent has contracted to perform. This is probably more common with complex medical needs of a pet-sitting assignment or the pet sitter has a family emergency. In such situations, the Agents should agree on a mutually acceptable split of the total pet-sitting fee.

Either arrangement tends to show that the Agent, not the hiring company, controls the methods and means by which the work will be performed, because, as with an Agent's right to hire assistants, the Agent retains the right to decide who will perform the contracted-for work.

The Agent's and the Company's Compensation

It is **very** important that the Agent be paid for the completed pet-sitting job, either by a flat fee or a percentage fee negotiated prior to the performance of the Agent's services. Payment by the hour, or by monthly salary, should be avoided entirely. Employee benefits – such as vacation, holidays, sick leave, pension and profit sharing, health insurance, life insurance, etc. – are strictly for employees. Therefore, an independent contractor should not earn or accrue employment benefits of any kind.

But simply saying that the Agent should be compensated according to a flat fee or a commission may not be enough, either. In most independent contractor/Agent relationships, **the hiring company negotiates the fee** for the pet-sitting services with the client, and then pays the Agent's flat or "split" fee out of the fee received from the client. Since the Agent's fee is dependent on the price negotiated with the hiring company, it supports an argument that the hiring company has retained an important measure of control.

In structuring the compensation system, one should consider the services being provided by the respective parties. Are the parties charging for, and being paid for the services they are actually rendering? In the typical Agency, the hiring company refers a pet-sitting assignment to an independent contractor/Agent accepts or rejects the contract. The Agent meets and/or speaks with the customer and pets; the customer gives the Agent the instructions, reviews the dates of services, gives the customer their phone number, negotiates the charges and actually performs the pet-sitting assignment.

However, the typical compensation arrangement used by the Agency does not correspond to the services performed by the company and the Agent.

To make the compensation system fit the services actually being provided by the respective parties, **the Agent should charge the client** a fee for the pet-sitting services. In other words, the Agent should agree to perform the pet-sitting services **for a fee to be paid by the client, not the company**. After the fee is received from the client, the Agent should then turn in the customer invoice, contract and bill for their services to the Agency. One fee should be charged to the agent for the agency referring the assignment and a separate fee for the use of the company's forms used by the Agent to perform the services.

The Agent who signs a pet-sitting contract is responsible for the contracts contents, fees and instructions.

The Agent's fees for certain pet-sitting services will normally be established in advance of the referral so that the Agency can publish a fee schedule or quote the Agent's fees to clients. Fees for more specialized services can be negotiated by the Agent and the Agency prior to the Agent's acceptance of the particular pet-sitting assignment, or when the need for the specialized services arises.

Billing the Client for Pet-Sitting Services

Of course, the hiring company should not be expected to give up the security that comes with billing and receiving payment from the client. By performing that function, the hiring company is assured, at the very least, that it will get paid if the client pays the bill.

The hiring company can protect its interest in getting paid, even though the Agent has a direct fee relationship with the client, by providing the Agent with billing services on all assignments referred by the company. Of course, the company should charge the Agent for these services, since billing services are overhead items.

The Agent should present the pet-sitting company with a copy of the invoice for services rendered when the finished pet-sitting contract is done, as an independent businessperson would normally do. The hiring company should then prepare and send another bill to the client. After receiving the fee from the customer, the company should prepare a reconciliation showing the total fee received, subtracting the company's fees for referral, billing services and any other items, and paying the net fee due to the Agent.

Payments to independent contractors/Agents should be treated like any other vendor account payable; i.e., payment should be made at the same time and from the same account as other vendors. Agent fees should not be paid on the same schedule as are employee wages (i.e., on regular weekly, bi-weekly, or twice-monthly paydays) or from the company's payroll account. Payments to Agents from a payroll account or on weekly, bi-weekly or twice-monthly paydays may be construed as evidence of an employment relationship.

Workers' Compensation Insurance

If a valid independent contractor relationship exists, the hiring company does not have an obligation to provide workers' compensation insurance coverage for the Agent, and the hiring company is usually not responsible for any injuries suffered by the Agent during the course of performing services under contract to the hiring company. However, if the Agent has been incorrectly characterized as an independent contractor, and the hiring company has not carried workers' compensation insurance on the Agent, the Agent/employee would have a right to sue the hiring company in civil court for damages suffered due to injuries sustained by the Agent during the course and scope of his duties. Usually, damages for such injuries are not covered by an employer's general business liability insurance policy.

Avoiding a Continuous Relationship

An employer-employee relationship is almost always continuous in nature. The employee works day-in, day-out for an employer for months or years on end. On the other hand, independent contractor relationships are usually infrequent or non-continuous in nature, with the independent contractor generally being hired to perform one assignment at a time. When the assignment is completed, the contract for services usually terminates also. Thus, the longer and more continuous an independent contractor's relationship with a company, the more it begins to look like an employer-employee relationship.

This does not mean that an independent contractor cannot provide services to a company more than once. But the hiring company should make it clear that the contractual relationship between the parties begins and ends with each pet-sitting assignment.

The independent contractor agreement between the parties should either set out a definite duration (the shorter the better) or state that although the agreement sets forth the general terms which will govern each assignment, each pet-sitting assignment creates a separate contract with the Agent. Further, the written agreement should provide that the company has no obligation to offer any particular pet-sitting assignment to the Agent.

The company should also encourage the Agent to perform pet-sitting work for the Agent's own clients or for other pet-sitting companies. Requiring an Agent to work exclusively for one company ties the Agent's fortunes so closely to those of the company that a court or taxing authority may be inclined to conclude that the relationship with the Agent is continuous in nature.

Reconciling the Right to Discharge and The Right to Terminate

The right to discharge is a right retained by an employer to fire an employee. In common law, and according to California Labor Code Section 2922, an employer has the unqualified right to discharge an employee with or without cause and with or without notice. That right rarely, if ever, exists in other business relationships. It is your responsibility to be aware of your state right to discharge and the right to terminate laws.

On the other hand, the right of termination is the right of a party to a contract to end the contractual relationship for reasons stated in the contract, upon giving an agreed period of notice, because one party has breached the contract, or because of other legally recognized reasons. As is discussed above, the contractual relationship between the Agent and the hiring company may be structured so that it automatically terminates when a pet-sitting assignment is completed. Since most pet-sitting assignments are completed in a rather short time period, it would rarely be necessary to terminate the contractual relationship with an Agent during the term of the contract.

If the written agreement is for a term, the parties may choose to decide that either party has the right to terminate the agreement upon giving a reasonable notice, usually two weeks or more. Every written agreement should provide that the agreement can be terminated immediately for breach.

The hiring company should also insist on a clause holding the Agent responsible for damages incurred by the hiring company if the Agent abandons or fails to complete an assignment he or she has previously agreed to perform. In the absence of such a clause, an argument can be made that the Agent does not have a legally meaningful obligation to perform the agreed-upon services, and that the Agent's relationship is therefore akin to that of an employee.

Federal Safe Harbor Rules

For federal income tax purposes, if the hiring company fails to prove that an Agent is an independent contractor under the IRS "20 Factor" test, all is not lost. Congress currently provides that if the hiring company demonstrates that it acted **in good faith** when it mischaracterized the employee as an independent contractor, **the IRS must waive any assessments for back taxes, interest and penalties** that would otherwise be owed for failing to withhold taxes, etc., from the mischaracterized Agent's pay. Congress refers to this special waiver rule as the Internal Revenue Code Section 530 "Safe Harbor".

It is important to understand that the "Safe Harbor" rule applies only to federal employment taxes. There is no comparable "Safe Harbor" rule for state employment taxes.

Further, the "Safe Harbor" rule only comes into play *after* the IRS or a tax court has concluded that one or more alleged independent contractors are actually employees.

In order to qualify for the "Safe Harbor" waiver, the employing company needs to meet three main requirements:

1. The hiring company must not have treated the Agents as employees at any time during the period in question.

2. The company must have correctly filed all of the required IRS returns, including information returns, during the period in question. These returns include, but are not limited to *IRS Form 1099*.

3. The employer must establish a *reasonable basis* for treating the Agents as Independent Contractors. In determining whether the hiring company has a reasonable *basis* for not treating an Agent as an employee, the IRS has acknowledged that reliance on any one of the following "Safe Havens" is reasonable:

4. Judicial precedent or published rulings, whether or not relating to the particular industry or business in which the hiring company is engaged; or IRS technical advice, an IRS letter ruling, or an IRS determination letter which specifically pertains to the hiring.

5. A past IRS audit (not necessarily for employment (tax purposes) of the hiring company, if the audit entailed no assessment attributable to the hiring company's employment tax treatment of individuals holding positions substantially similar to the position held by the individual whose status is at issue.

6. A long-standing recognized practice of a significant segment of the industry in which the hiring company was engaged (the practice need not be uniform throughout an entire industry).

There is an important caveat that the hiring company must be aware of when seeking "Safe Harbor" relief. If the company (or a predecessor) has treated any Agent, or any worker holding a substantially similar position, as an employee for employment tax purposes for any period of time after December 31, 1977, the company *cannot* take advantage of the "Safe Harbor" protections. This means that the company must have consistently treated *all* workers performing pet-sitting services as independent contractors. However, "Safe Harbor" relief will not be denied under the "consistency" provision for any periods prior to the periods in which the individuals were treated as employees.

However; the IRS, California courts and administrative agencies, have long recognized that a corporate officer or manager can treat himself/herself as an employee with respect to certain duties, and as an independent contractor with respect to other duties. To do so, however, the administrative work and the pet-sitting work must be treated as separate transactions.

Independent Contractor Records

The following items should be in the Pet Sitters file.

- W-9 verification of Taxpayer Identification Number signed
- References (Pet Sitting Related)
  (Names, address, phone numbers)
- Resume
- Signed Independent contractor agreement
- Copy of Fictitious Business Name Application
- Copy of Business License
- Copy of Certificate of Bond
- Business Cards
- Copy of Invoice for Billing
- Copy of all 1099 forms you file reporting your payments to the IC.
- Copy of any State forms you may need to report payments to the IC.
- Each State may require a New IC or Employee form to be filed. The State of California requires DE542.

Keep your Independent Contractor files for at least six years.

A Model Agreement

Now that you have some understanding of the legal principles and how they apply to your business, you are in a much better position to understand, utilize, and modify your needs. The agreement incorporates the principles from the prior chapters.

The written agreement can and should serve as the cornerstone to a successful independent contractor relationship. To this end, the agreement should clearly define the parties' expectations and relationship to one another. It is imperative, however, that the agreement be an accurate reflection of the relationship. Even if the agreement is a beautifully crafted instrument that contains all of the magical wording that should be in a proper independent contractor relationship, it is not worth the paper it is printed on if it does not reflect the parties' true relationship.

Example: you may have a provision in your agreement that expressly states that the pet-sitter can set his/her own hours of work, or that the pet-sitter is responsible for all methods and means to perform the work. However, if that agreement does not accurately reflect the parties' working relationship, any court or administrative body that is reviewing the relationship will give virtually no weight to the agreement. Thus, it is imperative that the agreement accurately describes your relationship with your pet-sitter(s).

The purpose of providing the model agreement below is to provide pet-sitting agencies with the framework for establishing a legally defensible independent contractor relationship. However; the model agreement is just that, a model. It is not designed as a "one-size-fits-all" document. As a result, the model agreement may not fit your own business practices, or it may not be to your liking for many other reasons. As a result, you may need to make some changes to the agreement, and review those with your own counsel to confirm that the changes conform to independent contractor legal principles and your individual work situations.

Independent Contractor's Master Agreement for Pet-Sitting Services

INDEPENDENT AGENT AGREEMENT

This Agreement is made between. .... (Agency) and .... (Agent) The Company and the Agent wish to enter into an agreement which sets forth the terms and conditions which will apply in the event that the Agent agrees to perform pet-sitting services as an independent contractor for clients of Agency in the future. Therefore, Agency and Agent agree as follows:

COMMENTS TO INTRODUCTORY PARAGRAPH

This section of the Agreement is intended to set forth information about the parties themselves and their individual intentions in entering into the Agreement. If the language used to describe the parties is not accurate, please revise it accordingly, keeping in mind, however, that the idea is to set the stage for establishing the Agent's independent nature.

1. SERVICES

AGENCY links clients who need their pets cared for while they are away from home, with professionals who provide at-home care for domestic pets, and related services. AGENT desires to perform such services for such Agency's clients. The SERVICES are expected to include, but are not limited to, providing pet and plant care in the residence of customers, inspecting client's grounds, and collecting mail and newspapers for clients ("Services").

COMMENTS TO PARAGRAPH NO.1

This paragraph provides a general overview of the services that will be provided.

INDEPENDENT CONTRACTOR

AGENT is a skilled pet-care professional who is equipped with training, equipment and other necessary tools to perform Services in the pet-sitting industry. AGENT acknowledges that he/she is not employed by, nor seeks employment with AGENCY, and that no employee/employer relationship exists, or is inferred or implied by this agreement. The parties understand and agree that AGENT is an independent contractor with respect to the performance of his/her duties and obligations hereunder.

COMMENTS TO PARAGRAPH NO.2

This paragraph provides a general statement about the independent nature of the pet-sitter. More importantly, it also sets forth the parties' expectations regarding their relationship – namely, that both parties intend to be in an independent contractor relationship.

3. ASSIGNMENTS

AGENCY may offer AGENT the opportunity to perform Services for AGENCY customers. AGENCY is under no obligation to offer any particular assignment to AGENT and AGENT shall be free to accept or reject any assignment proposed by AGENCY.

COMMENTS TO PARAGRAPH NO.3

Remember that the right to control is the most important element that a Court or administrative body will review in determining whether an independent contractor relationship exists. This paragraph establishes that the company has the option to offer assignment(s) to the pet-sitter, and that the pet-sitter retains the right to accept or reject any assignment which is offered. This reinforces the fact that the company cannot control the agent's decision whether to work or not, which negates one major element of an employer's control.

The fact that the agency is also under no obligation to offer any Agent a particular assignment reinforces the fact that the parties do not necessarily have a long-term relationship. Recall from the previous discussion that an ongoing long-term relationship can be a factor indicative of employment.

4. PERFORMANCE OF SERVICES

For each assignment accepted, AGENT shall perform the Services requested in accordance with the instructions of the client. AGENT will obtain the instructions, either written or oral, directly from the client. AGENT shall be solely responsible for the time and manner in which the Services are performed.

COMMENTS TO PARAGRAPH NO.4

This paragraph describes the Agent's obligation to perform the work based on the instructions of the client, not of the Agency. It also provides that the Agent can utilize and establish his/her own methods and means of performing the work (so long as it conforms to the client's instructions). This is intended to establish that the Agency is not controlling the Agent's performance of Services if he or she accepts a pet-sitting assignment. The requirement that (1) the Agent abides by applicable laws and an industry standard of practice, (2) receive direct client approval, (3) meet client specifications, including time deadlines, and is all intended to establish that the company is not exerting "control" over the Agent's work. The Agent also reserves the right to control the methods and means of his or her own work. Finally, the Agent's performance is only complete when the client, not the company calls to say they are home and accepts the pet-sitting invoice, once again removing control from the company.

The AGENT reserves the right to hire employees or to subcontract with other independent contractors/AGENTS to assist AGENT in the performance of Services under this Agreement. However, those employees or subcontractors must be approved by the client and meet the qualifications set forth in section 5 below. Hiring employees or subcontracting to another AGENT shall not in any way affect the AGENT'S obligations under this Agreement.

5. QUALIFICATIONS

Bonding: AGENTS must be bonded by a commercially reputable bond or insurance company ("Honesty Bond"). AGENCY must be named as an additional insured party. (An up-to-date copy of the certificate of such bond will be attached to this Agreement). Continued coverage and timely renewal of such bond is required during the duration of this Agreement.

Insurance: AGENT must be insured by a commercially reputable insurance company for liability arising out of the performance of such Services ("Liability Insurance"). (An up-to-date copy of the certificate of such insurance will be attached to this Agreement). Continued coverage and timely renewal of such insurance is required during the duration of this Agreement.

Self-Employed Status: AGENTS performing Services for AGENCY are self-employed, independent AGENTS. Thus, a copy of Fictitious Name Application, Business License certificate, business card, or any other similar document shall be provided to AGENCY and attached to this Agreement.

6. NON-EXCLUSIVITY AGREEMENT

Nothing in this Agreement shall prevent the AGENT from providing pet-sitting Services to any other person or entity, provided that doing so will not interfere or conflict with the AGENT's duties and obligations under this Agreement.

RECORD-KEEPING AND EXPENSES

Records: AGENT shall maintain an accurate account of the Services performed (AGENT'S INVOICE). At the end of each assignment, AGENT shall deliver promptly to AGENCY one completed copy of the AGENT'S INVOICE.

Expenses: AGENT is solely responsible for any and all costs and expenses incurred by the AGENT, or the AGENT'S employees or subcontractors, during or coincident to the performance of Services under this Agreement. It is anticipated that the customer shall provide all necessary pet, plant care and/or housekeeping supplies and equipment. However, if the customer fails to do so, AGENT'S expenses for such supplies shall be the responsibility of AGENT.

7. CONTRACT FEES

Customer Billing: All Services rendered by AGENT shall be billed directly to the customer by the AGENT. AGENT is permitted, but not required to use AGENCY'S preprinted invoice and statement. AGENT shall endorse to AGENCY any check received by AGENT, AGENT's employees or subcontractors from a customer for AGENT's performance of Services hereunder.

AGENT'S Service Fees: AGENCY shall treat AGENT'S invoices for fees in the same manner as it treats invoices from all other creditors. Accordingly, AGENCY shall make payment to AGENT once every month, on approximately the 15th day of each month. Payments will be based on each paid customer billing received by AGENCY at least one week before each invoice payment date. AGENT shall receive 50% of the amount actually billed and received from each customer pursuant to the invoice submitted to Agency. Any refunds or fee adjustments made to customer by AGENCY will be charged back to AGENT, and AGENCY shall have no liability to the AGENT for any fees billed to but not received from a customer.

8. STATE AND FEDERAL TAXES

AGENCY shall not make deductions, contributions or withholdings for local, state, or federal taxes from the AGENT'S net fee. Agency will not withhold FICA (Social Security and Medicare taxes) form contractors' payments, or make FICA payments on Contractors behalf, or make state or federal unemployment compensation on Contractor's behalf, or withhold state or federal income tax from Contractor's payments. Contractor shall pay all taxes incurred while performing Services under this Agreement, including all applicable income taxes and, if Contractor is not a corporation, self-employment (Social Security) taxes. Upon demand, Contractor shall provide Agency's with proof that such payments have been made. AGENCY shall file Federal Form 1099 and State Form equivalents, on all amounts paid by the Company to the AGENT, and shall provide the AGENT with copies thereof.

10. WORKERS COMPENSATION

Agency will not obtain workers' compensation insurance on behalf of Contractor or Contractor's employees or contract personal If Contractor hires employees to perform any work under this agreement; contractor will cover them with Workers' compensation insurance and provide Agency with a certificate of workers' compensation insurance before the employees begin the work.

11. UNEMPLOYMENT COMPENSATION

Agency shall make no state or federal unemployment compensation payments on behalf of Contractor or Contractors employees or contract personnel. Contractor will not be entitled to these benefits in connection with Services performed under this Agreement.

12. TERM

This Agreement can be terminated upon the mutual consent of the parties, or by either party for a material breach of any of the terms.

13. NON-COMPETITION

AGENT agrees that during the term of this Agreement and for a period of one year immediately following the termination of this Agreement, AGENT shall not, directly or indirectly, make known to any person, firm, or corporation the names or addresses of any of the customers of AGENCY or any other information pertaining to them. AGENT shall not call on, solicit, or take away, or attempt to call on, solicit, or take away any of the customers of AGENCY whom AGENT contacted or became acquainted with during the term of this Agreement, either on AGENT'S behalf or on behalf of any other person, firm, or corporation. AGENT further agrees that upon termination of this Agreement, AGENT will promptly return all customer accounts, reports, belongings, keys, and other records relating in any manner whatsoever to the customers of AGENCY, whether prepared by AGENT or otherwise coming into AGENT's possession.

14. LIMITATION ON AUTHORITY

Neither party shall have the right to bind the other by contract or otherwise, except as specifically provided by this Agreement. The AGENT shall have no authority to sign any document on behalf of AGENCY or in any manner whatsoever, without the prior written authorization of AGENCY. This agreement shall not be construed as a power of attorney.

The AGENT shall not hold himself/herself out to the public or to clients as an employee or AGENT of AGENCY. When engaged in performing Services under this Agreement, AGENT may hold himself/herself out to the public or to clients as an independent, professional pet-sitter with whom AGENCY has contracted to perform Services.

15. LIABILITY/INDEMNIFICATION

The AGENT assumes any and all liability for the death or bodily injury of any person or pet, or damage to any property, including but not limited to the person or property of the customer, the AGENT, the AGENT'S employees, subcontractors, guests, or invitees, arising out of the AGENT'S performance of Services under this Agreement.

AGENT agrees to indemnify, defend and hold AGENCY harmless from any and all claims, demands, and liabilities, including costs and attorneys' fees, to which AGENCY is subjected as a result of any act or omission of the AGENT, or the AGENT'S employees or subcontractors, during or attendant to the AGENT'S performance of Services under this Agreement, or arising in any other manner, or at all.

AGENT shall be liable to AGENCY for any losses or damage suffered by AGENCY as a result of the AGENT'S failure to properly complete the assignment, unless the AGENT was unable to do so because of the circumstances beyond the AGENT'S control.

16. NOTICES

All notices required or permitted by the terms of this Agreement may be given in writing by first class mail, postage prepaid at the addresses indicated below.

17. GOVERNING LAW

This Agreement shall be governed by and construed in accordance with the laws of the State of California, and the venue for any action relating to this Agreement shall be Contra Costa County, California.

18. INTEGRATED AGREEMENT

This Agreement is a complete expression of the parties' agreements and supersedes all prior and contemporaneous agreements, understandings and practices, whether oral or written. This Agreement may not be modified except in a writing signed and dated by both parties.

19. ATTORNEYS' FEES

The prevailing party in any court or administrative litigation to enforce or interpret the provisions of this Agreement shall be entitled to recover reasonable attorneys' fees and costs incurred in the prosecution or defense of said action, in addition to any other relief to which that party might otherwise be entitled.

20. SEVERABLE PROVISIONS

If any provision of this Agreement is finally held by a court of competent jurisdiction to be void or unenforceable for any reason, then the same may be severed from this Agreement without affecting the validity or enforceability of the remaining provisions of this Agreement, which shall remain in full force and effect.

21. ACKNOWLEDGMENT

AGENT acknowledges that he/she has read and understands this Agreement, and has had the opportunity to consult with an attorney or other experts of his or her choosing in determining whether or not to execute this Agreement.

Agency of Smithville   AGENT: ....
Pet & Home Services   Address: ....
P.O. Box 622   ....
DeSoto, CA 94522   ....

(xxx) xxx-xxxx   Telephone: ....

Dos and Don'ts

From the Hiring Company's Point of View

Step	Action
1.	When initially contracting for work, make it clear to the Agent that he is an independent contractor, not an employee.
2.	The parties should have an agreement stating that they are creating an independent contractor relationship. Most importantly, the parties must **abide** by the terms of that agreement.
3.	Do not give the Agent, and do not require the Agent to follow, any instructions on how to perform the Agent's services.
4.	Do not require the Agent to submit progress or interim reports for your review.
5.	Do not provide training for the Agent.
6.	The company should never refer to itself as the Agent's employer.
7.	Do not require the Agent to work at a certain job location. This means, do not require her to be at your office at certain times, on certain days, etc.
8.	Do not require the Agent to clear days off with the company.
9.	Do not require the Agent to work exclusively for your firm.
10.	Encourage the Agent to work for other firms, or his own clients.
11.	Beware that if the company has employees who do work which is substantially similar to the work of the company's independent contractors/Agents, the company will not be eligible for "Safe Harbor" status.
12.	Do not pay for the Agent's expenses or the Agent's tools, instrumentalities and materials.
13.	Do not require the Agent to use the company's materials.
14.	The Agent should be responsible to provide his own insurance, etc.
15.	Do not forbid the Agent from hiring assistants.
16.	Do not force the Agent to hire assistants.
17.	If the Agent hires assistants, their wages and costs should be paid by the Agent and not the company.
18.	Pay the Agent only by the job and not by any other means, such as hourly, daily, etc.
19.	The Agent should not accrue any benefits characteristic of those commonly received by employees (i.e., vacation pay, holiday pay, sick leave pay, overtime pay, retirement and profit sharing, health insurance, etc).
20.	The company should consider carrying workers' compensation insurance for the Agent, on a cost reimbursement basis.

Dos and Don'ts

From the Agent's Point of View

Step	Action
1.	Present yourself to the public as an independent Agent for hire.
2.	Establish an office in your home, or in another place of your choosing, and furnish it with your own office supplies.
3.	Have business cards describing yourself as an **independent** agent printed, at your expense, in your own name, and not just in the name of the agencies with whom you contract.
4.	Take out a business license in your own name, or in the name of your own business.
5.	Take out a separate business telephone at your home or your own offices.
6.	Set up a separate bank account for your business.
7.	Maintain a set of books and ledgers for your own **independent** contractor/Agent business.
8.	List yourself in the white pages or, better yet, the Yellow Pages of the phone book as an *independent* pet-sitter.
9.	Engage in marketing and advertising efforts on your own behalf.
10.	Work for more than one shop, if possible.
11.	Negotiate your fee on a per-job basis and not by the hour, day, etc.
12.	You should not receive any benefits from the company, other than your negotiated fee.
13.	Do not represent yourself to clients, property owners or the general public as an employee of the company, but rather as an independent contractor who contracted to perform the service.
14.	Decide for yourself where you want to perform your work.
15.	Set your own work hours.
16.	Provide, at your own expense, the tools and materials that you need to do the job.
17.	If you hire assistants to do a pet-sitting assignment, you are responsible, not the company, for their pay, workers' compensation insurance, tax withholdings, etc..
18.	Carry insurance to cover yourself for liabilities caused by you or your assistants because, as an independent business person, you are liable for your own acts and omissions.
19.	Always think of yourself as an *independent* business person.

Common Law Factors Used to Determine Workers' Classification

Note: It is up to you to keep current on all IRS & state rulings that might change or add to these factors.

The IRS uses 20 common law factors to determine whether workers are employees or independent contractors (see *Internal Revenue Manual 4600 Employment Tax Procedure, Exhibit 46401*). Workers are generally employees if they:

1. Must comply with employer's instructions about the work

2. Receive training from or at the direction of the employer

3. Provide services that are integrated into the business

4. Provide services that must be rendered personally

5. Hire, supervise, and pay assistants for the employer

6. Have a continuing working relationship with the employer

7. Must follow set working hours

8. Work full-time for an employer

9. Do their work on the employer's premises

10. Must do their work in a sequence set by the employer

11. Must submit regular reports to the employer

12. Receive payments of regular amounts at set intervals

13. Receive payments for business and/or traveling expenses

14. Rely on the employer to furnish tools and materials

15. Lack a major investment in facilities used to perform the service

16. Cannot make a profit or suffer a loss from their services

17. Work for one employer at a time

18. Do not offer their services to the public

19. Can be fired by the employer

20. May quit work at any time without incurring liability

How to Meet the Twenty Common Law Factors Determining Workers' Classification

With the use of Independent Contractors make sure that you do NOT CONTROL the manner and means of how the contract is taken care of.

Below is an example of how you can meet the twenty common law factors.

- The pet-sitter meets directly with the client, takes all information about the services to be performed. The price for the service is determined at this time. Agency does not get involved in this step.

- Pet-sitters do not receive mandatory training.

- Pet-sitters do provide other services that are integrated into the business. Pet and home services are part of what Agency sells.

- Pet-sitters do provide services outside of Agency.

- The pet-sitter is not prohibited from providing similar services to other third parties. The only restriction is that the pet-sitter not solicit former and existing

Agency clients for separate work; this is an appropriate protection of a customer list and trade secret.

- Most pet-sitters pay a three percent (3%) fee to use Agency forms and bonding when servicing a customer who contacted Agency. This is a matter of economics and choice for the pet-sitter.

- The pet-sitter selects any employees or subcontractors that he/she wishes to use. The pet-sitter is responsible for all applicable taxes, insurance, etc. Agency' legitimate interest in approving the individual selected is to assure a continuing level of quality and competence in performing the services, to protect the Agency name.

- No pet-sitter of Agency may hire, supervise, or pay assistants for Agency services.

- The average length of time for which a pet-sitter accepts a contract through Agency is three days.

- The pet-sitter sets the time for work with the customer. Agency has no input on this.

- There is no guaranteed regularity or continuity in work provided by Agency. The pet-sitters set their own hours, handle their own expenses, and use their own tools.

- The advance notification of unavailability is given so that Agency may tell a customer a particular pet-sitter will not be available if the customer should telephone for service.

- Pet and home care is provided for the client in the clients' home, not on Agency' premises.

- The pet-sitter determines his/her own time to report for work and the time that work will cease.

- Pet-sitters do not submit regular reports to Agency.

- Services are performed by the pet-sitter on a per-project basis, rather than on an hourly basis.

- All expenses incurred by the pet-sitter in connection with the operation and conduct of the pet-sitter business, including but not limited to supplies, equipment, automobile expenses, and subcontractor or pet-sitter's employee expenses, shall be paid by the pet-sitter.

- The pet-sitter provides his/her own tools, such as flashlights, scoopers, extra pet food, etc. There is a suggested list by Agency for this "kit," but it is not required, nor checked by Agency. The pet-sitter uses his/her own transportation.

- No facilities are needed for a pet-sitter to perform services.

- The pet-sitters pay an administrative fee for the services of Agency in screening calls and customers. Further, there is a risk to the pet-sitter that his/her time will not be profitable, if Agency cannot collect the fee due within 90 days. In such event, the contract provides for an adjustment to the contract fee paid to the pet-sitter.

- Pet-sitters are not prohibited from working for others, and the majority of the present pet-sitters use the fees they receive to supplement their income. Pet-sitters are also attracted to the work because they enjoy handling pets and plants, and the ability to do as much or as little work as they choose.

- The contract can only be terminated for material breach or upon five (5) days written notice.

- The pet-sitter is expected to finish any uncompleted jobs regardless of danger of illness, or death of an unattended animal.

Additional Items that may be used in determining Classification of Workers

1. SKILLS REQUIRED

Pet-sitters must demonstrate pet skills, including the administration of medication, the handling of different types of pets, recognition of illness, basic first aid, and knowing how to handle an emergency. In addition, pet-sitters must show self motivation, time-management capabilities and communication skills.

2. CUSTOMER BILLING

The pet-sitter collects the fee for the service directly from the customer and provides a receipt to the customer. If the customer does not pay prior to receiving the services, the pet-sitter bills the customer.

3. REPLACEMENT OF LOSS

All expenses incurred by the pet-sitter in connection with the operation and conduct of the pet-sitter's business, including but not limited to supplies, equipment, automobile expenses, subcontractor or employee expenses, and replacement of any loss, damage or injury to property or pet(s) while in the care of the pet-sitter, shall be paid by the pet-sitter. It is anticipated that the customer shall provide all necessary pet and plant supplies.

4. PRICING SET BY PET-SITTER

Agency should only quote a price range to the customer. The pet-sitter must set her own price, which sets the pet-sitter's rate of pay.

Independent Contractor Reporting

Any business that is required to file a form **1099MISC** must also report certain information to the STATE about any independent contractor services to the business. Independent Contractor information must be reported to the State of California Agencies EDD department within 20 days of making payments to contractors of $600 or more.

The information required is:

BUSINESS INFORMATION

- Federal employer I.D. number
- Social security number
- Business name, address, phone number

IC INFORMATION

- First, middle, last name
- Social security number
- Address
- Start date of contract *
- Amount of contract *
- Contract expiration date *

    *This information may not be applied with each filing

FAQ's

Throughout this guide, the point is made that it is not enough for the parties to see themselves as Independent Contractors. They must also continually strive to reinforce the independent contractor relationship in their dealings with one another. During the course of their relationship, Agents and hiring companies will undoubtedly encounter criteria's that relate to the factors discussed in the previous chapters. How you deal with these criteria's will likely affect a court's or administrative agency's determination of an Agent's status. This section will help you respond to selected criteria's.

Criteria No. 1 *An Agent requests the hiring company's permission to (a) take the day off or (b) take a vacation.*

Response: The Agent is an independent contractor. The hiring company's approval of days off or vacation time is not necessary. As an independent contractor, the Agent sets his or her own hours of work. The company's only concern is that the Agent complete pet-sitting assignments within the time deadlines set by the client.

Note: Do not take or threaten to take adverse action against the Agent for taking time off from work, for refusing to accept assignments, for not reporting to work at the company's offices, etc. Doing so indicates that you have the right to control the Agent's working conditions.

Criteria No. 2 *The Agent wants to be paid by the hour, by the day, or on a basis other than payment by the job, because they do not think it is fair that they are not paid for all the time they put into a pet-sitting service request.*

Response: Advise the Agent that as an Independent Contractor they have the discretion to decide when to work, which assignments to accept, and how long to spend on each assignment. These are the benefits of being an independent contractor. The downside of the relationship is that they are not guaranteed a profit. Therefore, it is up to the IC to use their time efficiently so that their efforts produce an acceptable financial return.

Criteria No. 3 *The Agent wants to accept contracts with another pet-sitting company and seeks your permission to do so.*

Response: Advise the Agent that it is not necessary to obtain the company's approval. As an independent contractor, they have the right to work for anyone they choose, including competing pet-sitting services. Typically, Agents should market their services to the general public so that they can perform pet-sitting work for other companies and their own clients. Working for multiple companies is a strong indicator of independent contractor status.

Criteria No. 4 *The agent refuses to accept a distant pet-sitting assignment unless the company agrees to pay for his travel, meals and lodging.*

Response: The hiring company should refuse to pay for the Agent's expenses. As an independent contractor, the Agent is responsible for the incidental expenses incurred in performing contracted-for services. The Agent can, however, take the estimated costs of travel, meals and lodging on a distant job into consideration when negotiating his fee for the assignment. When the Agent accepts the assignment for an agreed sum, it is the Agent's responsibility to pay for their own expenses and to keep those expenses to a minimum to maximize their profit potential on each assignment.

Criteria No. 5 *What if the Agent turns down an assignment?*

Response: Do **not** threaten the contractor for not accepting the assignment and do **not** withhold future assignments because they turned down the assignment. Offer the assignment to another contractor. Use the opportunity to reinforce to the Agent that they have the right to reject assignments because they are an independent contractor.

Criteria No. 6 *What if the Agent asks for permission to hire an assistant?*

Response: Advise the Agent that, as the hiring company, you do not have the right to tell the Agent who they can hire. As an independent contractor, the Agent can hire anyone to assist them complete the pet-sitting assignment, as long as they produces a contract and invoice which satisfies contracted-for requirements. Of course, the Agent has the sole responsibility to pay and supervise their assistants.

Criteria No. 7 *Assume that the Agent uses the hiring company's offices and market research data to perform assignments. What action should be taken if the Agent refuses to check into the office each day?*

Response: The Company should not require an Agent to report to their offices at any certain time. As an independent contractor, the Agent works on their own behalf and the company should only be concerned with receiving an acceptable contract and invoice. How they achieves that result, and the resources used to do so, are unimportant.

Criteria No. 8 *After a contract or invoice has been provided to a client, the client calls the hiring company to ask questions or complain about the contents of the contract or invoice. What should the company do?*

Response: Assure the client that you will relay their concerns to the Agent, who will take care of them. Then contact the Agent, explain the client's concerns, and remind the Agent that their performance, under the contract with the hiring company, is not complete until the client is satisfied with the Agent's contract or invoice, and that you expect the Agent to satisfy their contractual obligations.

Criteria No. 9 *The agent states that they are no longer going to accept pet-sitting assignments from the hiring company.*

Response: Check your written independent contractor agreement to see if the Agent has a right to terminate the agreement at that time or for the stated reason. The Agent has a contractual obligation to complete pet-sitting assignments previously accepted. If the Agent refuses to complete an assignment they previously agreed on, and the hiring company sustains a loss as a result (*example:* a customer is dissatisfied and no longer gives the hiring company work), tell the Agent you will hold them responsible for the loss.

Criteria No. 10 *The hiring company is not satisfied with services being performed by an Agent and wants to fire them immediately.*

Response: The Company does not have the right to fire an independent contractor during the term of the contract. But the company may have a right to terminate the contract if the Agent has failed or refused to perform important aspects of their contractual obligations. *Example:* if the Agent told you that they were not going to be available to complete the contract, even though a previously accepted assignment was due in one week, the company would have the right to terminate the contract for that assignment and to contract with another Agent to perform the assignment. Of course, the hiring company could also take into account the Agent's history. *Example:* failing to complete contracted-for assignments, turning in pet-sitting reports which did not meet contract specifications, in deciding whether to offer future pet-sitting assignments to the Agent.

Criteria No. 11 *The agent encounters a difficult problem with a pet-sitting assignment and asks the Agency owner for help in performing the assignment.*

Response: There is nothing inappropriate when two independent professionals discuss/brainstorm an interesting problem. Professionals in various fields frequently look to their peers for guidance, as a matter of professional courtesy. However, a careful balancing act is required to ensure that neither party crosses the line between *a brainstorming session* between two independent professionals and a Agency owner giving instructions or advice to an employee/Agent on how to perform a pet-sitting assignment. Giving instructions on the methods to be used to perform an assignment could be seen as evidence of control. If the problem cannot be resolved easily, the Agency owner should consider entering into a fee-sharing or subcontracting agreement with the Agent.

101-C: Workbook to Running a Successful Pet Sitting Business

Part 3
Marketing and Advertising

Marketing and Advertising

Marketing and advertising are key components to starting and maintaining a successful pet sitting business. This section is intended to assist those who start a pet sitting business and how to introduce themselves into the community as well as maintain a superior reputation. These methods are not a guaranteed ticket to success, but by using them I have continued to run a reputable and successful business since 1981!

As you prepare your marketing materials remember to do it with a clear understanding of what your customer wants and to show them how you will provide it. As you build your client base, listen to what your customers need and prefer. You just have to ask them and listen to their feedback. The best marketing programs are created by customer's feedback and shared with everyone who represents your company.

Making the Phone Ring

Marketing

The first step in developing your Marketing and Advertising Campaign is to prepare your start up costs and determine your yearly advertising budget. To help you determine your yearly budget this chapter lists different forms of advertising and useful tips that will help you reach your prospective customers. Your start up cost should include a budget for the creation of your logo and the artwork for your promotional materials. Having a distinctive logo that people will remember is very important. I do not recommend skimping on what will be the first impression of your business. All marketing materials should present a clear picture of the services you have to offer. On the following pages you will find a sample brochure to get your creative juices flowing. Your marketing and advertising plan should be as well diversified as a stock portfolio. Your logo should be a simple design and your name catchy so they are easy to remember and recognize. As you read about the many marketing avenues, rank each one based on which fits your budget, time and abilities.

Launch Business Website

Getting Started:
- Get your own domain name and register it for several years.
- Get a decent host. Pay the extra dollars for a unique IP address
- Set up email address using your domain.

- If you do not know how to make a great website either hire a web designer, join House Calls to have your own website and be part of an established site or go with a simple back ground color, fonts and real life pictures. Remember the website will be the first impression of your business to online potential customers.

What to put on Home page:
- Make sure your business name, what you do, where you do it, who you do it for and why you're the best appear on the home page. Make it short yet descriptive.
- Your business mailing address, phone number with area code and email address should appear on every page.
- Cities you serve in your local area.

Other pages you should have:
- About page
- Services page
- Contact page

Make your website search engine friendly:
- Make sure the tags an each page are unique and include some keywords you think people would type into a search engine to find your site.
- Make sure meta description tag on each page contains a sentence that serves as a mini-advertisement for your company that makes people want to find out more as it may appear at times under the title of your website in Google and other search engines.
- Add some links to your website that are useful to people looking for information about your services.

Online promotion of your website:
- Get your business listed with Google Maps:
  https://www.google.co/local/add/login

- Get your business listed with SuperPages.com:
  https://my.superpages.com/spweb/products/business-listing

- Get your business listed with Yahoo Local:
  http://searchmarketing.yahoo.com/local/business.php

- Get your business listed with MSN local via localize.com:
  http://www.localeze.com/manage/

- Get your business listed with local.com:
  http://www.local.com/advertise.aspx

- Get your business registered with the local search engine at BOTW:
  http://local.botw.org

- Update your business listing with infoUSA.com
  http://listusa.com/dbupdate.htm

- Update your business listing with Acxiom
  http://bcb.acxiom.com/start.pl

Promote your website offline:
- All Marketing materials: (Advertisements, brochures, flyers. Business cards)
- Add to Email signature

BROCHURE AND BUSINESS CARD

Your business card and or brochure could be the first impression of your business! It is important that these materials be well written, attractive and indicative of your professionalism.

A good brochure should contain information about what your service provides, the advantages it offers, how it works, and probably, how much it costs. Tell your customers what you are selling in large print. Your logo and name should be easily recognized.

Let's review a sample brochure:

Sample Brochure Front

(Company Name)

Pet Sitting Services

Since Year

Bonded

Insured

Licensed

"Worry-Free Travel"
Kennel Alternative

1(888) 888 – 8888
Web Page

Keep the information simple, easy to read and understand.

Sample Brochure inside left Fold

Step-by-Step Pet Calls

STEP 1…

Call us

We will match our services to meet your needs.

STEP 2…

Your personal Sitter will call you to:

–set a meeting with you & your pets in your home
–determine the best routine to ensure your pet's comfort and your worry- free travel.
–prepare your individual instructions

STEP 3…

While you are away

Your personal instructions are followed. The typical call consists of:

–bringing in the newspaper & mail
–feeding the pet
–spending time playing with and/or exercising the pets
–scooping the yard and/or litter box
–a security check before locking up

*Service continues until you call to say you're home!

State how you offer what your potential customer wants in simple easy to read terms.

Sample Brochure inside Middle

PET CARE

Love and Attention

Food and water

Exercise and daily walks

Scoop maintenance

Quality time

Prescribed medications

HOME CARE

Security Check

Daily home inspection

Mail & newspaper pickup

Garbage/recycling set-out

Plant/yard/garden care

Grocery shopping

The Average charge is $---- per visit to your home.

Sample Brochure inside Right Fold

$ 5.00 OFF

| (Company Name) |
| Pet Sitting Service |
| Phone number |
| Web Page |

* 3 consecutive days or more required. Not valid with any other offer.

Sample Brochure Back

Name
P.O. Box XXX
City State 22222
www.yourname.com

Potential Customer

Address

City State Zip

** Remember to know your state laws on the classification of workers. In the state of California pet sitting companies that use Independent Contractors are sometimes classified as referral agencies. (CA code 687.2) This code has specific requirements about how they want referral agency to be placed on all forms of advertising!

The Personal Touch

The most inexpensive, impressive and long lasting forms of advertising are the ones that personally reach out to the people who can spread the word about your business. The most effective way to accomplish this is to personally promote your business yourself. Consider beginning your advertising campaign by personally promoting your pet sitting business at the following places:

- Veterinarians
- Pet Stores
- Groomers
- Travel Agencies
- Apartment Complexes (that allow pets)
- Humane Societies and Non Profit Pet Organizations
- Local Businesses and Companies

Building a list of places to visit is easier and cheaper than ever! I have listed several resources to help you purchase or personally create your marketing lists. Place your list in a spreadsheet format to save time and available for multiple uses. You will be able to create personalized introductory letters, special mailing offers and more! The list ideally includes the name of the place, addresses, phone numbers, email addresses and the contact person.

MARKETING LIST

Company	Contact	Address	Phone	Called	Meeting	Mail	Follow Up

Describe Your Business

Before you begin calling the marketing sources you have gathered describe your business in twenty-four words or less. Practice saying your business description out loud until the flow of words are in the correct order and comfortable to say. Next, practice on friends and family members for confidence building.

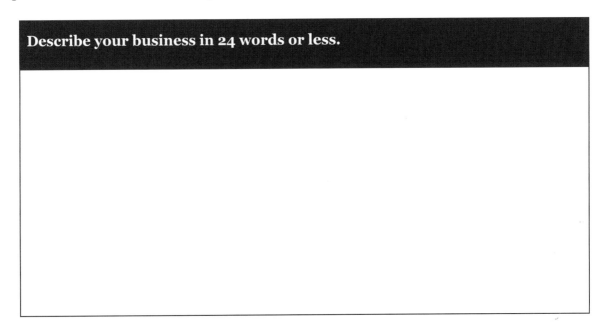

Describe your business in 24 words or less.

Believing, Communicating

With your marketing list created and your business description complete you are ready to schedule the dates and times that you are dedicating to begin your marketing campaign. Create a quite location where you can sit by the phone comfortably and not be interrupted. Dress professionally, place your spreadsheet with extra paper and pens on the desk or table and take a few deep breaths.

Calling:

- Veterinarians
- Pet Stores
- Groomers
- Travel Agencies
- Apartment Complexes (that allow pets)

Introduce yourself (Name and Company), describe your business in twenty-four words or less and ask to speak to the appropriate person from your list.

If they are available:

Introduce yourself (Name and Company), describe your business and let them know when you are out in the neighborhood and that you love to stop by and meet them. Ask what day and time would be best for you to drop by to introduce yourself. If they do not have time ask if it would be okay to drop off your business card and or brochure with a special introductory offer for their employees and clients.

Find out who would be the appropriate person to give your company packet to and if they have a location for you to place your business cards and or brochures that is easy for their customers to see.

Always, deliver your advertising packets by hand to Veterinarians, Groomers, Pet Stores, Travel Agencies and Apartment Complexes (that allow pets)!

Calling:
- Humane Societies and Non Profit Pet Organizations
- Local Businesses and Companies

Introduce yourself, describe your business in twenty-four words or less and ask to speak to the appropriate person from your list.

If they are available:

Introduce yourself, describe your business and let them know when you are out in the neighborhood and that you love to stop by and meet them. Ask what day and time would be best for you to drop by. If they do not have an appointment offer to mail them your business card and or brochure with a special introductory offer for their employees, members or clients!

If they are not available:

Ask what the best time is to call and reach them and place this time in your appointment book.

Prior to making your marketing rounds review "Know How to Network" mentioned later in this book and remember that the receptionist may hold the key to the door to future business relations with this source of potential customers.

VETERINARIANS, PET STORES & GROOMERS

- Make monthly visits to form a cooperative relationship! Bring snacks for the staff to show your gratitude.

TRAVEL AGENCIES

- Offer a special discount to the employees when they travel.

APARTMENT COMPLEXES

- Apartment complexes provide a welcome-packet of information to new residents. Inquire about adding your brochures to their front desk.

HUMANE SOCIETIES AND NON PROFIT PET ORGANIZATIONS

- Volunteer to help with special events they may be hosting.
- Offer discounted services to anyone adopting a pet through these organizations.

LOCAL BUSINESSES AND COMPANIES

When you obtain a list of the major employers in your area, the contact person is usually the head their Human Resource Department. You will want their name and phone number. Often benefits managers in these departments are on the lookout for services and information that will be useful to their employees. They may print a blurb about your service in their company newsletter, or post your brochure on employee bulletin boards, or in the company cafeteria.

Note: Some Chamber of Commerce Business listings are available online!

CIVIC CLUBS AND NONPROFIT ORGANIZATIONS

If you're comfortable with public speaking, offer to give a talk about your new business at their club's next meeting. If you are in need of public speaking skills and you would like to improve your skills consider taking a speaking course offered by your local community college or community center. Have your friends attend and sit in the front row!

FRIENDS AND FAMILY MEMBERS

Get your brochures to those who know you and will support you in your venture. Everybody knows or works with someone who has a pet, and that someone may be interested in using your services. A personal recommendation means a lot in this business, so get your friends and family members to spread the word about your unique service.

DOG WALKS & PET SPECIALTY SHOWS

Cities are organizing dog walks and pet specialty shows. Many are held at the county fair grounds or at your local city park. Rent (or make) a cute animal costume, then attend, handing out your brochures!

CANVASSING YOUR NEIGHBORHOOD

Turn your brochure into a door hanger with plastic bags. Map out neighborhoods that you would like to offer your services to. Distribute the hangers every other month for one year, and watch the results!

COMPANY CLOTHING

Opportunity exists in the grocery store – wear your Pet Sitting T-shirt and/or a name tag. WEAR THEM ALL THE TIME! People read these, and you'll be amazed at the number of times people will inquire about your occupation. Store clerks, waiters and waitresses, post office personnel . . . these are just a few who will ask about your pet- and home-care services simply from reading your badge or clothing.

SEIZE ALL FREE OPPORTUNITIES

Watch for pets! Keep your brochures and business cards with you at all times; you never know when you may need them.

*You must reach a potential future client six times to become part of their subconscious with an easily recognizable logo and company name. This must happen in order for them to think of YOU when they are looking for a pet sitter.

Know How to Network

Networking can lead you to a wealth of information to put to use in the present and a world of resources you can rely on in the future.

You can join many organizations to network your business. Look in your local small business newspaper for a calendar of local clubs' meeting times and places. Visit several in your area to find the one which best fits you.

Develop a plan for how you will build relationships and how you can share your story briefly!

Family, friends and neighbors can be a great networking source. Let them know what you are up to in business so that they can network for you!

The key to social networking is activity. You need to be regularly active and that activity needs to provide benefit to other members of the community. By doing this you can effectively promote your website and generate more traffic to your website.

Wear your name tag over your heart, and have your business cards in your left pocket. Shake hands firmly with your right hand, make eye contact and pull your business card out of your pocket with your left hand. Be sure to ask open ended questions of the other person. Having a memorable conversation requires being a good listener. Stay in contact with the most meaningful contacts.

Remember the Value of N E T W O R K I N G . . .

N   *Remember Names.* When you meet someone, repeat his or her name in conversation. It compliments the person and helps you remember what he or she is called.

E   *Make Eye Contact.* Looking at someone sincerely and directly is the best way to connect with him or her quickly. Nothing is more awkward than trying to talk to someone who's looking over her own shoulder or around you instead of at you.

T   *Talk and listen more.* Instead of chatting about yourself, ask other people questions. "Effective networking is about quality, not quantity." Listen to people's stories – you never know what you might learn from them.

W   *Write a follow-up note.* Stay in touch with the people you connect with by sending them a short note after the meeting. Thank them for their time and mention something about the conversation that you found helpful.

O   *Be Open.* Keep an open mind about people. After all, even if they can't help you, you never know to whom they might be able to refer you. Also, ask open-ended questions in conversation, like, "What brings you to this meeting?" or "How did you get started in this business?" Probe for answers. The more information you get them to share, the more likely you'll learn something helpful or interesting.

R   *Be a Resource.* Too often, people use networking as a chance to get rather than to give something. Offering assistance or advice to people will make them remember you in a positive light.

K   *Knowledge is power.* That goes for everything – people you meet, or companies you might do business with. Research on the Internet. Read, read, read ~ industry publications, newspapers and newsmagazines. Carry a small notebook to jot down newsworthy items to ask people about. You might ask their thoughts on anything – say, the presidential campaign.

I   *Take Initiative.* Involve yourself. Be proactive. At events, go up and talk to people instead of waiting for them to come to you. Just remember to let them do most of the talking!

N   *Be Nice.* "Networking is about cultivating relationships." "'What goes around, comes around,' so treat people with genuine courtesy." To do otherwise gives networking a bad name.

G   *Set a Goal.* Goals need not be big. If you're shy, tell yourself that at the next event, you'll introduce yourself to just one person and you'll follow up with a phone call or note afterward.

Networking Websites:

Social networking is one of the biggest phenomenon's to hit the Internet there are many sites that you can use to promote your business and becoming an active and useful member of these communities will help increase exposure for your website and business.

- LinkedIn: LinkedIn site is geared solely towards professionals and businesses. It is structured so that when you add a new member to your list of connections, it also adds their connections to your list and the connections of their connections. This helps you build a mammoth list of new contacts to greatly improve your exposure.

- Facebook: Is not solely towards professionals and businesses. It does attract a more mature audience with a slant towards business relationships. The unique features and opportunities, including Facebook marketplace and applications make it a powerful addition.

- Reddit: These social bookmarking website members can add stories, news pieces and articles that are read by others and bookmarked if they are good. He more pieces you submit and the more bookmarks you receive the greater your exposure.

- Squidoo: Social bookmarking website. It has an added feature that enables registered users to answer nagging questions posted by other users, promoting your profile as an expert in a field.

- Youtube: Helpful to be successful in social media optimization or virtual marketing. Videos can be instructional, informational, educational, humorous or a commercial.

Diversify through Media

One way to reach large numbers of people with your advertising message is through the social media, newspaper, radio and television stations.

Create a Media Spreadsheet of all social media, newspapers, radio stations and television. Look for small local newspapers in your community. Many homeowner associations, private complexes and apartments have newsletters that are more economical to advertise in. Include the source of media, addresses, phone numbers, email addresses and the contact person. Call and ask for an advertising packet to be mailed to you prior to meeting with an account executive. This packet should include demographics and rates for a wide variety of advertising rates available to you.

NEWSPAPER

To get the most for your buck you need to run your newspaper ad several times throughout a year. By committing to an annual newspaper advertising budget your local paper may offer you a discount. You can put a variety of advertising options together.

- Classified Ad Under "Pets"
- Special Seasonal Pet Sections
- Small Display Ad

WHEN TO ADVERTISE

Run the newspaper ads on Sunday through Wednesday to get better response. More people tend to travel Thursday through Saturday and miss the daily paper. Primarily, advertise before holidays, during the summer vacation months, and on the anniversary date of your business opening.

CREATE A FEATURE STORY

Free publicity will give your new company creditability, name recognition and start your phone ringing. Take your new company brochure, business card, a short informal informative letter stating your back ground with pets and how long you have been a member of your community with a picture of you with your pets personally to your local newspaper, television and radio stations. Introduce yourself, state what your service offers in twenty four words or less and ask if they have a reporter who might be interested in writing an article about your business. Follow up with a phone call to determine if any of the media is interested in interviewing you about your new service from either a human interest or business angle. If they bite and put you on the local evening news, this is valuable free advertising most small business owners otherwise could rarely afford! These stories do promote your business credibility.

Radio

Advertising through radio has different strengths and weaknesses. It targets a select audience, it reaches this audience efficiently, and there is more time to get the message across. Since there is no visual message, though, it does not receive full attention, unless it is run numerous times.

Request Arbitron ratings from several stations to determine which groups listens to what radio station and when they listen. Arbitron periodically publishes these demographic statistics about the listeners for each station. Once this information is gathered, you can most effectively determine the right station and time to place your commercial.

When to Advertise

Monday, Tuesday and Wednesday would be the best days to reach the vacationers before they leave town. Compare morning and evening rush hour traffic prices.

Television

Virtually everyone watches television! Television advertising is a lot more affordable than I had imagined. Each station's sales representative worked with me to find our target viewing audiences. Watch your local cable TV and talk with the station about commercial possibilities. Network television stations need heavy repetition! They do deliver to a large audience. I found that the small local TV station that airs community events, high school sports, town news and Chamber of Commerce meetings are the most economical. The local stations are a powerful advertising tool to help build your company reputation with the movers and shakers of small towns.

When to Advertise

Repetition! If you decide to make television part of your advertising packet, commit to one year. Ask about annual coverage of special events that might relate to your business and special pet related shows.

MOVIE THEATER

Run business ads prior to showing the coming attraction so that you can capture the audience as they wait.

Your logo and name will flash before their eyes several times before the movie, making your logo a part of their subconscious just like McDonalds! When I tried this, everywhere I would go people said, "I saw you at the movies!" Committing for six months to a year was not as pricy as you would think.

WEB PAGE

The web page, shown contains detailed information about you and your business, as well as giving customers the ability to request service, will be very beneficial to your business. Include your web address on all forms of company advertising and stationary.

A domain name is a very important part of people finding your web page. There is not much of an available pool of domain names anymore, so one must be creative and try not to spend too much time thinking of one. Some sites provide a free domain name search tools.

Make sure that you search the .com, .net and .org extensions. If the name you choose is available, the site will give you information on how to register it. There is also a link to a starter site web hosting service that will help you to create a web page under your domain name. This will be the first impression of your business for some potential clients. It would be wise to have a professional create your site.

Having your business name exactly match your domain name is ideal but may not be possible. There are several things you can try to make sure that your company name is still similar to your domain name. You can try shortening it, adding hyphens between the words, adding "Corp" or "Inc" at the end if that applies to your business, etc.

YELLOW PAGES

The Yellow Pages has given me a constant steady source of new customers for my business. Today people are automatically drawn to my familiar logo. My ad drives people to my Web Site for further information twenty four hours a day! Call your phone company about Yellow Pages advertisements ask for a first time customer discounted rate.

COUPON MAILINGS

Being part of a direct mailing piece you can save money and time while reaching potential new customers. Coupon books are easier for the customer to cut out and save for their future needs. Collect all direct mail advertisements that you receive and shop advertising rates and distribution routes of the ones that you feel might be best suited for your needs. Call a couple of the advertisers of service related business and ask about their whole experience dealing with the company and customer response.

DIRECT MAILING

Direct Mail, or advertising mail, is a proven cost-effective way to find new customers, the increase in customer loyalty, and to drive sales.

By putting out a direct mailer you will:

- Encourage interest in new product or service
- Generate sales
- Drive traffic to you
- Generate leads
- Announce promotions to valued customers
- Increase recognition

Direct Mailing Piece should include a logo, name, phone number and web address. Make sure your message to the prospective customer states what you are offering them in a short simple message. Select something catchy that will grab attention. Be creative! Empower your marketing message by reaching your customers with unique formats that demonstrate your product and encourage responses.

While you are creating an eye catching mailer that increases your effectiveness you must determine who your targeted market is. Tuesdays is the lightest mail delivery day.

Building an effective mailing list is easier and cheaper than ever! First, base your mailing list on specific customers (i.e.: large companies (CEO, Human Resource manager), Home Owners, (age, income, marital status, pets, hobbies), specific Business Owners (veterinarians, Groomers, Travel Agencies etc...). There are Government Programs designed to help you find your targeted market mailing list and much more. They are funded by your tax dollars.

The United States Postal Service:

www.usps.com/directmail

You can even find reputable list brokers who can advise you on what type of list would best work for you. Many of these brokers can build list based on your specifications.

Small Business Development Centers:

www.sba.gov/sbcd

You can acquire expertise and advice at no charge on a large variety of small business issues. They have access to targeted mailings, which it can offer you at an economical rate.

Additional resources

Internet Directories:

www.google.com

You can research and build lists for free! Look for a useful directory on the Web that features your targeted customers. Locating your local of Chamber of Commerce, Trade Associations, Volunteer Organizations and Welcome Wagon can be found easily on the internet.

Homeowner Associations

You can scout the neighborhoods that fit your profile and then find out which associations manage those subdivisions. Upscale associations have monthly newsletters that will allow inserts or ads for a smaller fee than local newspapers and the postal service.

Satisfied Customers

Positively Exceptional Service creates satisfied customers and sets a small business apart from its competition. Strive to do business on a personal level. The best form of advertising your business is to have a client who praises your services. Although word-of-mouth advertising may take longer to give your business a boost, it's still the greatest advertising around. To motivate clients to tell others about your business, leave your business card on their counter on your last visit with a note explaining your $5.00-off referral discount towards their next service request, plus $5.00 off for their friend. At the very least, send a thank-you note for their recommendation of your service. Ask your customers for feedback on everything. What is it that your customers do not like? Strive to improve or correct your business practices. Never forget above and beyond positive interaction and service will keep your customers coming back.

MEASURE RESULTS

Track how every potential customer and customer finds you. This can be done by using a computer program. This report should run monthly to determine which marketing programs are working the best.

With each inquiry find out how the potential customer found you and record this information in a manner that will allow you to have this information readily available for making future advertising decisions.

I have created a "referred by" report in my computer program to determine how clients have found out about my services each month. The majority of my clients learned about my services from these sources:

- Customer Referrals
- Veterinarians
- Yellow Pages
- Internet
- Movie Theater
- Web Page
- Direct Mail
- Company Referrals

Part 4
Day to Day Operations

Introduction

This Section of the book provides help with organizational and prioritizing ideas and examples to get your office up and running on the right foot each day. To save time you can computerize with all the items below and more!

HouseCalls4Pet.com   *101PetSitting.com*

Space:

The Office location was discussed in Book 1.

Set regular office hours:

AM to PM, BUT always have an emergency number!

Will your office be quite and free from interruptions? Is your office in your home? If so have you had a family, spouse and/ or roommate meeting to discuss how you need them to conduct themselves if they are at home during your business hours? Communicate with everyone you live with. Share your goals and objectives? This would be the perfect time to share what times will work for everyone to have dinner and or breakfast together. Everyone can be supportive of each other and feel that they are important. Running a company from home requires everyone being flexible, informed and involved. Creating a daily time line will help everyone stay on track!

Hours you are In Office

Whether you are using a computer or not you should have a paper trail. Daily back ups one the most important tasks at the end of each office day.

The following will show you samples of the forms I have used in my pet sitting business, after each sample will be a page with explanations of each item on the previous form. Below you will see each step of how I organize my office time to reach key objectives.

Be Flexible!

You should be in the office prior to your advertised office hours to set up and take care of the phone lines. You must have this time to organize, retrieve messages, and find out who called to say they are home.

Before answering phones organization

- Turn on your computer.

- Have sharpened pencils and erasers ready.

- Message Books (duplicate, spiral bound & four messages per page)

- Retrieve email, phone messages (look each customer up client and their usual pets sitters name on existing clients message), note all informational messages, make a message of which clients were do home that you have not heard from yet.

- Handle any emergencies, note all pet sitters who have not confirmed that they received your messages from the day before, reassign any customer that any pet sitter does not wish to accept.

- Sort messages; informational, emergencies, bookings, prospective new, repeat customer bookings, last minute requests.

- Return Phones Calls: Enter in scheduler while speaking to customer and place in pet sitters call pile.
  *Using a head set while on the phone has many benefits!

- Obtain the following information to pass on to pet sitter: Dates and type of service – Time leaving and returning – The customers emergency contact information.

- Assign to a pet sitter, let the client know that their pets are on the schedule and a pet sitter will call to confirm as well as gather any new instructional information or to set up and appointment to meet them and their pets and fill out the paperwork.

Invoices

Bookkeeping

Marketing

***Computer Back up**

Out of Office

    Pet Sitting Calls

    Banking

    Marketing

    Post Office

    Any other errands on your organized list

SAMPLE OFFICE TIME LINE PROCEDURES

8:30 *to* 9:00

- Turn on computer and retrieve messages.

- For repeat customers put client number and pet sitter name on each message, note any account balances and key status.

9:00

- Answer phones

(Do not put clients on hold for over two minutes take down their name and number and offer to call them back. Put them at the top of the call pile.)

- While answering the phones do the following in this order.

Sort messages

Schedule changes, Information, Agent & Client Messages

Call repeat customers

Enter bookings and/or changes for each customer in the computer and place in pet sitter message box.

Return **informational** *calls.*

If you leave a message, leave office hours.

If they want service & need a registration put their information in the computer.

Run last visit report

Make a message for each pet sitter that has a client due home and place in agent message box.

After these things are done, separate the things that need to be done during the week into something each day.

Monday:

- Run pet sitter schedules for Monday thru Friday
- Enter all contracts, invoices, checks & key information from the weekend.

Tuesday:

- Double check as well as clean out the pet sitter messages and make 15 registration packets.

Wednesday:

- Put in the next weeks weekly customers

Thursday:

- Run the pet sitter schedule for Thursday to Monday & run the past weeks pet sitter commission reports.

Friday:

- Balance the last week's commission reports and call pet sitters with messages.

Pet-Sitter Paperwork

Yes, making pet sitting visits means taking care of pets and homes when the owners cannot. It also means keeping track of scheduled contracts, customer instructions and keys, billings, payments and your commission. This section explains and gives examples of the forms your Agency business could use.

NOTE: The fees used in the examples may not conform to your area.

Customer Service Requests

Record the following information for each service request.

Date:
Write the date you received the request.

Name/Client Number
Enter the client's name and the account number.

Address:
Write the client's street address, town and the zip code.

Phone:
Record the client's home, cell and work telephone numbers and their emergency number if it is known at the time.

Dates:
Use this column to record the days you are scheduled to visit.

132

Visits:

Enter the number of visits per day, and the requested time.

No. of Days:

Write in the number of days you will make visits.

Total:

Tally the client's balance due

Pets:

For new clients, note the number and types of animals, e.g., 1 dog, 1 cat. For repeat clients, note any changes in the pet population, e.g., "Sammy died," or "new kitten." Changes in pet population may affect the rate you charge.

Client Confirmation:

Write the date on which you either spoke with the client or left a message on the recorder.

Registration/Meeting:

If you make an appointment to meet your client for a registration, key pickup, etc., write in the date and time.

Date/Time of Return:

Use this line when you confirm service requests from repeat customers.

Notes:

Add any other information the client gave you, such as a change in diet or medication. Know where your clients are going so you can add a personal reference to the note you leave on your last visit.

Service Agreement

This document is the basic contract between a client, the pet-sitter, and Agency. By signing it, the client makes warranties and guarantees regarding their home and pets, and their financial responsibility to pay for services. These services include those performed directly by pet-sitters, or contracted by them on the client's behalf in the event of a pet or household emergency.

Below is a description of the information needed for the Service Agreement.

Date:
Enter the month, day and year of the registration.

Pet Care:
Give a description of the animals in the household. Include the type (e.g., dog), name, sex, age, and breed or color. To save space, use abbreviations such as these:

A = aquarium
B = bird
C = cat
D = dog
F = female
M = male
DLH = domestic longhair (cat)
DSH = domestic shorthair (cat)

Key Disposition:
When a client instructs you to keep their keys on permanent file, check the box "Agency Retains" and sends or delivers duplicates to her office. If the client wants the keys returned after service

- *Complete the service request*
- *Check the "other" box*
- *Describe how and when the keys should be returned.*

Customer:
Mars this line as one of the two places the client must sign, and print their name on the agreement.

Note: As an authorized pet-sitter of the Agency, you should sign and print your name on the agreement after reviewing for completeness and accuracy.

To Veterinarian

This portion of the Service is to be used only in the event of a medical emergency, but must be signed by the client at the registration. Leave the name of the veterinarian and the description of the pets.

Customer Signature

Highlight the second place the client must sign and print their name on the agreement.

Note: When you complete the contract, give the pink copy to the client. Put the yellow copy in the client's file and send the white (original) copy to the office on the Monday following the registration.

Sample Service Agreement:

(YOUR NAME), Pet Sitting Services, Phone #

SERVICE AGREEMENT   Date: _____

(Your Name) or its Pet-sitter agrees to perform the pet & home care services pursuant to the terms and conditions of this Agreement and any additional instructions of Customer contained on the Customer Service Instruction Form attached hereto. Care of the customer's residence and following pets:

SERVICE AGREEMENT

This is a Long Term Agreement. The above described services shall be performed from time to time as requested by Customer and the charges therefore shall be at the rate in effect at the time services are requested. Charges are payable in advance of each request of service. This Agreement may be cancelled by Customer at any time provided 24 hour notice is given to (Your Name) or its Pet-sitter prior to and commencement of service date. In which event all amounts paid by Customer will be refunded less $_____ to cover administrative expenses. This Agreement may be terminated at any time by (Your Name) or it's Pet-sitter, in which event the advance payment shall be refunded in full less charges for all services actually performed pursuant to this Agreement prior to date of termination.

1. Customer additionally warrants, represents and agrees as follows, and this Agreement is entered into by (Your Name) or its Pet-sitter in reliance upon the following:

2. Customer has communicated to (Your Name) or it's Pet-sitter all defects, hazards, dangerous conditions, or other unusual circumstances on Customer's premises which would in any way affect the performance by (Your Name) or it's Pet-sitter of the above described services.

3. Customer has communicated all dangerous or unusual propensities or past occurrences of dangerous conduct on the part of any pets on Customer's premises.

4. Customer hereby agrees to indemnify and hold harmless (Your Name) or its Pet-sitter from any and all loss caused by any acts of Customer's pets.

5. Customer agrees to indemnify and hold harmless (Your Name) or its Pet-sitter from all liability from loss, damage, or injury to property or any pet in any manner arising out of or incident of performance of this Agreement, including without limitation all consequential damages, whether or not resulting from the negligence of (Your Name) or its Pet-sitters, except to the extend such damage is caused by willful misconduct or gross negligence of the part of (Your Name) or its Pet-sitters.

6. Customer hereby grants permission to (Your Name) or its Pet-sitters to enter Customer's premises at any time for the purpose of performing this Agreement.

7. Customer agrees that (Your Name) or its Pet-sitters shall exercise sole discretion in providing any medical attention which may appear to be necessary for the well-being of Customer's pets, in which event the customer agrees to reimburse, within thirty days, (Your Name) or its Pet-sitter for any and all expenses which (Your Name) or its Pet-sitters may incur as a result of providing such medical attention. (You're Name) or its Pet-sitter's time will be billed at the hourly rate in effect at the time services are rendered.

8. Customer agrees PAST DUE accounts are subject to a ten dollar fee and 1-1/2% interest per month on any balance remaining unpaid more than thirty days after date of balance. In addition Customer shall be responsible for all cost incurred including reasonable attorney's fee or collection agency fee should this matter be turned over to an attorney or collection agency for collection.

9. Customer agrees that for any returned check, customer will pay on demand to (Your Name) the sum of said returned checks, a $25.00 service charge, plus 1-1/2% interest per month accrued thereto, in the form of cash, money order or certified check.

Customer, or a person designated by Customer to act in Customer's behalf in the event any emergency condition should be encountered by (Your Name) or its Pet-sitter in the performance of this Agreement, may be contacted at the address and telephone number indicated on the Customer Service Instruction form.

I have read the foregoing and enter into this Agreement pursuant to its terms and conditions.

CUSTOMER/EMPLOYEER   **PET-SITTER/INDEPENDENT CONTRACTOR**
X   X

CUSTOMER SERVICE INSTRUCTIONS

The Customer Service Instructions form sets forth the service dates and charges for the client's registration and FIRST service request, and requires the client's signature.

After completing the form, ask the client to review the information and discuss any changes. Countersigns the agreement, leave the pink copy with the client, and put the white (original) copy into the file. Place the yellow copy in the client file.

The boldface type corresponds with the preprinted information blocks.

Client #:

Give each client a number exclusive to them. Place this number on all forms, including invoices.

Referred By:

There are several ways your new client might have heard about Agency. Accurately recording the "who, what, where, when and why" of a registration helps us analyze which types of marketing techniques are best.

- Clients and Vets: Give the name of the client or vet, and later write a thank-you note.
- Clients also receive a credit for each registration they recommend.
- Telephone Directories: Record the directory and the heading the client used. Use abbreviations, if necessary:

> **YP** Pacific Bell Yellow Pages
> **K** Dog & Cat Kennels
> **P** Dog & Cat Pet-Sitting
> **H** House-Sitter Services

Promotional Material:

If the client has a brochure, business card, newsletter, or coupon, ask where they found it (e.g., All-Pet Veterinary Clinic), or if it was received in the mail. In all cases, note which type of material the client has.

Insurance Co. /Policy #/Phone:

You will need this information in the event of physical damage to the home that needs immediate repair.

Veterinarian/Address/Phone:

To save time during registrations, compile a list of the vet addresses and phone numbers you most often use. When you register a client who does not have a regular veterinarian, ask permission to use one you know, such as your own.

Other Key holders:

Note the names and phone numbers of other individuals who might visit the home, or could be of help in an emergency. If a key holder lives in the community, get the address as well.

Pet Immunization/Medical History:

This information helps acquaint you with the pet's general health and may dictate what procedures you should take to protect your safety.

Lights/Drapes:

Ask if any lights will be on timers or not otherwise be used by you. Also ask if lights and drapes are to remain "as is," or changed daily.

Utility Valves/Gas, Water & Circuit Breakers:

Note the location and instructions for shutting off these utilities, and where any tools needed are kept.

Initial/Repeat Registration:

For new clients, check the "Initial Registration" box and enter the appropriate fee. For repeat customers who have moved or have significant changes in their pet population, check the "Repeat Registration" box. Repeat registrations cost less than initial registrations.

One Time a Day:

List the dates on which you will make visits once a day only, even if you are expected to make multiple visits on other dates. Clients often leave in the morning and return in the afternoon or evening, and so don't need two visits on the dates of their departure and return.

Two Times a Day:

Write in the dates you are expected to visit in both the A.M. and P.M. Note: although the form appears to specify a rate per visit, multiple-visit days (and live-in days) are charged per Diem and not per visit!

Holiday Charges:

On certain holidays, clients may be asked to pay a premium for your services

Weekly/Hourly:

Some jobs may be contracted by the week (e.g., daily dog walking) or the hour (e.g., grocery shopping).

Discount Type:

Agency' customers can receive discounts for three primary reasons:

Coupons:

These are issued by the company and distributed through mailings or by pet-sitters. Coupon discounts are valid when applied to three (3) consecutive days of service. Never apply this discount to the registration fee.

New Customer Referral:

Occasionally a client will refer a new customer to Agency BEFORE they have completed their own registration. In this case, deduct the referral credit here.

14 days or more consecutive days of service:

You may elect to give a client a 5% discount for a minimum of 14 days of service, but I do not give both a coupon and a percentage discount for the same service period, nor discount the registration fee.

Total Charge for Service Payable in Advance:

Highlight this line so her new client understands that payment in full for the anticipated service is requested now. If the client won't be leaving for several weeks, they may allow them to leave a check in the home for the service dates, but always collect the registration fee at the meeting.

Approximate Hour of Day Preferred / Date & Time Return:

Note the time of day your client prefers you to make visits, and the expected date and time of their return. Referring to the last paragraph of the form, reiterating the importance of the client's telephoning upon their return.

Date: _____   Client # _____

CUSTOMER SERVICE INSTRUCTIONS

Client: _____   City: _____ State _____ Zip _____

Address: _____   Sitter: _____

Res. Phone: _____   Referred By: _____

Bus. Phone: _____   Insurance. Co. _____ Tel. _____ Policy# _____

Emergency Phone: _____

Veterinarian: _____

Address: _____ Phone # _____

Other Key holders: _____ Phone # _____

Cats: Outside Only/ Inside Only/ (Inside/Outside)   Exercised: _____

Litter Changed: _____ Dates: _____   Birds Cage Change: _____

Pets Immunization up to date: _____   Medication: Type: _____ Dose: _____

Medical History 6 Months: _____   Times Daily: _____ Pet: _____

Pets Quartered: Full House / Outside Only / (Inside & Outside)

Notes: _____

Dogs' Diet: _____

Cats' Diet: _____

Other Pets' Diet: _____

_____

Pet Supplies Stored: _____

Home Services: Inside Water / Outside Water / Mail / Newspapers / Lights / Drapes / Garbage

Notes: _____

Utility Values:

Gas: _____

Water: _____

Initial Registration: _____ Repeat Registration: _____

One Time a Day $ _____ per visit

Dates: _____ X _____ = $ _____

Two Times a Day $ _____ per day

Dates: _____ X _____ = $ _____

Weekly _____ Hourly _____ Monthly _____ $ _____

Dates: _____ X _____ = $ _____

Discount Type: _____ (_____) (_____)

Total Charge for Service Payable in Advance $ _____

Approximate Hour of Day Preferred: A.M. _____P.M. ____ Date and Time Return: _____

Important Note: If you wish to extend routine service beyond your planned return, please call the office and arrange extension with Company personnel only. The extension will be billed when you return.

If catastrophe or calamity should delay you from returning and **prevent you** from telephoning to arrange an extension within 12 to 24 hours after the last scheduled visit (see above), the Agent will resume visits and care, and you will be billed at the rates listed above. Please telephone when you arrive home for the reasons outlined above.

X _____   X _____

Customer Signature / Employer   Pet-sitter Signature

©2002 Agency Inc.

Update Sheet for Repeat Customers

Besides new notes left by a customer, the UPDATE Sheet is your most accurate source of information, and is an important part of the professional appearance that makes the customers feel so comfortable. The categories written in boldface type correspond to information blocks on the UPDATE Sheet.

Prior Balance:
Note whether the client owes money or is carrying a credit.

Date & Time of Return:
Remind yourself when the folks are expected home.

Dates:
Enter the current service dates.

Last Visit:
Write the last date and time (A.M. or P.M.) you will visit during this service period. This is your reminder to leave a note, the invoice, and make sure the home is neat for your client's return, (usually done on the next-to-last visit, in case the client returns early.)

Customer:
Use the customer's full name as given on the Service Agreement.

Client #:
Enter the customer's account number (generated by your computer program).

Address:
Use the customer's street address, even if they use a different mailing address such as a post office box.

City:
Enter the name of the town or city.

Home/Work:
Record the telephone numbers. Specify whose work number is listed.

Keys:
Note the number of keys and the doors and locks they fit, or where keys are hidden. Specifically note LOCKS WITHOUT KEYS that should not be used, so that you do not lock yourself out. Check the box to show whether the keys will be retained or returned.

Alarm:

Write NONE, or the location, code and procedure to follow if an alarm is accidentally set off.

Duplicate key:

Enter the date you mailed or delivered the client's key to the office.

Pet-sitter:

Print your name.

Driving Instructions:

Use broad directions for well-known streets, and specific directions for neighborhoods. Your substitute pet-sitter may not come from the same direction as she, so simple "left" or "right" instructions may be backwards.

Special Instructions:

Note any unusual requests not covered elsewhere on the form.

Customer's Out-of-Town Location, etc.:

Write in the names of hotels or other guest accommodations and the phone numbers. For people on a cruise, you may need the help of their travel agent to contact them in an emergency.

PETS

Name

In each column enter the name of a pet or group of pets (e.g., an aquarium).

Type

Enter dog, cat, bird, fish, etc.

Color/Mark

Enter black lab, Irish setter, Persian, orange tabby, black/white DSH, etc. Include an individual distinguishing mark when there is more than one animal of similar description.

Sex/Age

Enter M or F, neutered or spayed. Give the animal's current age and approximate date of birth. Approximate an animal's birth month and year by subtracting the animal's current age from the registration date. Assign a birth date of 10/88 to Yuppie Puppy and 5/87 to Itty Kitty.

Supplies:

Note the location of food, litter, medical and other supplies you will need.

Feeding:

Record the types, times and amounts of food for each animal. Specify the weight of canned food because an instruction such as "1 can" may mean a can of 3 oz., 6 oz., 14 oz., or more.

Medication:

Enter the type, dosage and frequency.

Quarters:

Note whether animals are to stay inside or outside only, or may come and go, either through pet doors or at your discretion.

Exercise:

Enter instructions such as "walk each visit," "play ball in yard," etc.

Cat Litter:

Note the location of litter boxes and when they should be changed. Many customers will simply say "as needed." Note disposal instructions, i.e., "into bags," "flush," etc.

Dog Scoop Details:

Give the type and location of cleaning tools, and where wastes should be placed. Clean the yard daily.

Watering Directions:

Note the client's instructions for each of the areas listed. Write the dates when watering is expected and circles each date when done. This is especially helpful when sharing an assignment with another pet-sitter.

Mail:

Check the box if you are to bring in the mail. If the mail will be held at the post office, write "NO." Check the mail box the first few days to make sure the stop order is in effect.

Trash:

Check this box if the client's trash is to be placed at curbside. Note the pickup day. Put out the trash the day before its scheduled collection, and bring in the container when empty.

Package Slips:

This item reminds you to check the mail for notices of attempted deliveries. Arrange to accept the mail or packages, or have them held and delivered when the client returns.

Newspaper:

Check this box if you expect to find newspapers delivered. Note if delivery has been stopped, then calls the carrier if papers continue to come.

144

Sample Customer Update Sheet

PRIOR BALANCE: _____ DATE & TIME OF RETURN _____

CUSTOMER: _____ CLIENT #: _____

ADDRESS: _____

_____

CITY: _____

Contact Numbers: Home _____ Alarm: _____ WORK: _____

KEYS:

KEYS:☐   RETAIN:☐ RETURN:☐

DUPLICATE KEY IN OFFICE ☐ DATE:_____ SITTER:_____

DRIVING INSTRUCTIONS: _____

_____

_____

_____

SPECIAL INSTRUCTIONS: _____

_____

_____

_____

CUSTOMER'S OUT-OF-TOWN LOCATION:

_____

PHONE #'s: _____

Customer's TRAVEL AGENT: _____ PHONE #:_____

Pets

NAME						
TYPE						
COLOR/MARK						
SEX/AGE						
SUPPLIES						
FEEDING						

Invoices and Customer Payments

INVOICES

1. Prepares an invoice for each service request you perform, whether it results in a zero balance, a charge, or a credit.

2. Always fill in the customer's name, account number, and address, and the billing date (including the year). The billing date is the date on which you start the visits for any service contract period, or performs services such as registering a new customer, purchasing pet food, or making special trips to pick up or return house keys.

3. Leave the white (original) copy of the invoice with the customer. Place the yellow copy in the office for bookkeeping. Staple the pink copy on top of the Customer Service Request and places it in the customer's file.

CUSTOMER CHECKS AND CASH PAYMENTS

1. Review each check for the customer's name, address, and amount of remittance. Add or correct the address, if necessary.

2. On the face of the check, write the customer's account number.

3. Paper-clip (do not staple) the check to the yellow copy of the respective invoice.

4. If paid in cash, record the cash payment on the invoice, place the cash in an envelope, and paper-clip the invoice to the respective envelope.

Sample Invoice

(Name)...
Address...
City, State & Zip.....................................
Phone..
Date ....

Name: _____ #: _____

Address: _____

City, State & Zip: _____

Pet-sitter _____ Prior Balance _____

Date	Services	Charges		Credits		Balance	
Payment							
Balance							

Payments are due on the first day of service. *Additional charges are on return. Past due accounts are subject to a $10 late fee and 1.5% and 18% APR interest per month service charge will be added to the balance.*

COUPONS

1. Issue discount coupons to attract new clients. Coupons are distributed in many ways:

   - Newsletter insert
   - Direct mail
   - Delivery by pet-sitters to vet offices, pet stores, etc.
   - Handed out at a booth
   - Given to customers who refer new customers

2. If a client redeems a coupon, subtract the value of the coupon from the total charges due for the current service request.

3. Note on the invoice that a coupon was redeemed and write the following four items of information on the coupon:

   - Her name
   - Name of client
   - Service dates to which the coupon is applied
   - Where or how the client acquired the coupon

4. Paper-clip the coupon to the corresponding yellow copy of the invoice and check. Mail it to the office on the next Monday.

VET CARD

The vet card is a postcard that you complete at each registration. It has two purposes:

   - To tell the client's vet that your Agency or their pet-sitter is authorized to care for the animal named and that the client assumes the responsibility to pay for any veterinary care charges
   - To keep presenting the name of your Agency to the veterinary staff in hope of getting more of their own clients referred

1. Write the name of the pet and its description on the left side. The agent writes the full name and address, including zip code, of the client's vet on the right side.

2. Ask the client to sign on the line "OWNER," and print their name below it.

3. Mail or deliver the card to the vet after the registration meeting.

Thank-You Card

The thank-you card is a blank postcard. Use it to send a personal note of thanks to any customer, veterinarian or other business that has referred a new client to you.

Leaving the Customer a Note

The note is just to personalize your services even more. A note with a few words about the animal or any adventures is a great way to make your customer feel even more comfortable with your services. The only item of information you MUST put in the note is a reminder to call either you or the office when they return. Anything else you write is at your discretion.

Examples of notes from pet-sitter to customer

Observations of pet behaviors, eating habits, and health:

- "Rocco", was absolutely adorable! I kept telling him that I had two hands and I couldn't pet both him and "Itty Kitty" at the same time, but he would have none of it.

- Itty "Kitty" always finished her food, but she never ate while I was there. She was more interested in lap time and brushing than eating.

- "Rocco", was limping when he came in from the yard tonight. I pulled a foxtail from his right front paw and cleaned it with an antiseptic. Better watch him for a day or two.

- Observations about plants, the household in general, or anything unusual that happened:

  - Your house plant by the living room table has three new shoots!
  - What a thrill! On Monday morning I arrived to find toilet tissue festooning the walnut tree in front! I got most of it, but there's a bit at the very top that I couldn't reach.

Coding Keys

Customers' security is a top priority. Having a discrete coding and filing system for customer keys is necessary.

- Label and code keys as soon as you receive them.

- If a customer gives you keys labeled with their name and address, remove the tag and replace it with your own. You may use either labels that stick to the keys or paper tags on rings.

Here is an example of key-coding:

1. Write the client's last and first initial.

2. Write the Client Number.

3. Write a town or city code.

4. Write pet's name.

Use abbreviations to make a standard code only and then file the keys according to the client number, or alphabetize by last initial.

Paying your Independent Contractors

Through the cooperation of the pet-sitter having accurate paperwork and turning it in on time, commission checks may be drawn up in an efficient manner.

The commission of a pet-sitter of Agency is based on the contracts serviced and invoiced by the pet-sitter. The pet-sitter is mailed the commission checks no later than the 15th for the preceding work month. A work month ends on the last Saturday of each calendar month.

THE CALCULATION

The suggested commission is 60% of the fee charged by the pet-sitter for the pet- and home-care services performed by that pet-sitter according to the client's instructions.

ADMINISTRATIVE FEE

A suggested three percent (3%) of each commission, up to a maximum of $24 (3% of $800), is deducted as the pet-sitter's share of expenses.

CUSTOMER EXPENSES

For expenses that have been incurred on behalf of a customer (e.g., pet food), the customer is billed for the reimbursement of the pet-sitter.

COMMISSION CHECKS (Weekly Calculations)

- Pet-sitters are responsible for billing the clients for the services performed.

- Pet-sitters are responsible weekly for submitting to the Agency office all checks collected, invoices, and a tally of invoices (a bill to Agency) from the previous week.

- If a pet-sitter does not turn in their invoices for each customer along with a bill to Agency (tally of invoices percentage), they are phoned and notified that their commission check CAN NOT BE ISSUED until all of their customer invoices for the current commission period are received.

- Computer printouts of weekly/monthly commissions for each pet-sitter are run every week.

- Run the commission report for the prior week and match it to the tally of invoices.

    Note: The computer report is based on the invoices provided by the pet-sitter and posted to the client's account.

Follow these simple rules to efficiently handle your invoicing and payables.

- Check for any differences between the pet-sitter's tally and the printouts of the tally of invoices submitted.

- Check for discrepancies against invoices – the tally of invoices and computer printouts should match.

- Keep the amount paid and dates the same in the computer. Make sure you do keep the amount paid and the date the same, so that you do not throw off your deposit.

- Arrange the bill of invoices according to respective pet-sitters in alphabetical order and staple each of the pet-sitters' bills together.

- If the invoices and tallies still are not equal, call the pet-sitter for clarification. If it is the pet-sitter's error, she will need to provide a revised invoice

- File in monthly commission folder.

COMMISSION CHECKS (Monthly Calculations)

1. Set a beginning and ending date for each commission-check period. They can be calculated from the first Sunday to the last Saturday of each month.

    Note: Remaining days in the current month are added to the commission check for the following month.

2. Compile all the weekly commission computer printouts and pet-sitters' weekly balanced bills for the commission period through the last Saturday of the current month.

3. Verify that all clients have been billed by looking in the computer under "Weekly/Monthly Tally Report & Pet-Sitter Bill."

4. Make sure new client contracts for each registration completed are in the office and fully completed by pet-sitters.

5. Call the necessary pet-sitters about all clients who have balances owing and have not been billed and/or have not paid.

6. Verify the correct monthly total due to the pet-sitter by adding the appropriate **weekly calculations together.** Print the monthly commission report and compare it to the weekly bill of invoices totals.

7. By the 13th of each month, a check is written in the agreed amount and attached to the monthly commission total statement. On the check, in the memo section, write a note stating, "Invoices through the (date = last day of the commission period)."

Sample of One-Week Tally Sheet for Paying Independent Contractors

ONE-WEEK BILL TO Agency

Record only from your invoices your commission for each day for Sunday through Saturday, in alphabetical order of clients. Do not mix weeks. Do not record until the week is complete. Mail by Mon. or deliver by Tues. of the following week. Check column "I" for invoices. L = last E = expenses. Send in revised invoices for any client invoicing changes. * = Substitute pet-sitter; explain in notes.

Pet-sitter …………………………….. Week of………………………………

E	CLIENT (NAME & # IN ALPHA)	S	M	T	W	TH	F	S	TOTAL
	TOTAL								

NOTES:………………………………………………………………………………………………

The Independent Contractor may use abbreviations in the weekday blocks, and may explain any additional billings (e.g., for an unscheduled visit or expenses charged back to the client) under Notes. The Independent Contractor totals their commission for each client in the right-hand column and their commission for each day along the bottom row. The sum of the numbers added in the vertical and horizontal "Total" areas should be equal.

Business Performance

The purpose of the following questions is to help you determine the performance of your business so that you will have benchmarks to grow from. Sometimes a business owner can be so busy working at the day-to-day operations of the business, they lose their vision. The following section can help you continue to stay focused on your key objectives.

1. What percentage of revenue will you invest in growing your business during the first 12 months?

2. What is your goal for gross revenue for the next 12 months?

3. What will be the average charge per pet sitting visit?

4. How many visits at the average charge will you need to make each day, to reach your gross revenue goal?

5. How will you track your business referrals?

6. How will you know what the average customer spends per year?

For Coaching contact DJ at:

http://HouseCalls4Pet.com

http://101PetSitting.com

10444247R00096